# PEOPLE OF THE WORLD

## Paul Burkhart

I0463514

PEOPLE OF THE WORLD

Paul Burkhart

ISBN    978-1-300-66416-1

Inquire:   peopleoftheworld3000@gmail.com

Facebook.com/peopleoftheworld3000

People of the World is an effort to catalog bizarre and/or interesting specimens I see on the streets of San Francisco, Los Angeles, and various other places. A couple of the drawings were inspired by events in my teenage years.

I have been astounded and disgusted by people since I can remember, and they become more tragic, vile, and beautiful the more intently I observe.

There is no way this project could ever be considered finished, but here is a collection of my favorite drawings from the series with their original captions and mistakes intact. The excellent drawings of my con-conspirator Jessica Vohs are not included here but will hopefully be published soon.

Paul Burkhart

OFF TO MARTHA AND BROS COFFEE
IN NOE VALLEY ON HIS TINY BIKE.

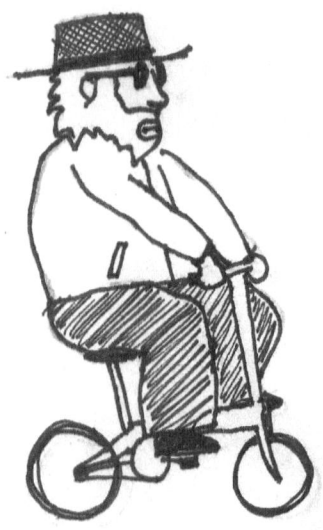

PAUL B. 6/2

Everything bright fluorescent
work-out gear. Bleached
mohawk.
FEEERTH.

Paul
7/20

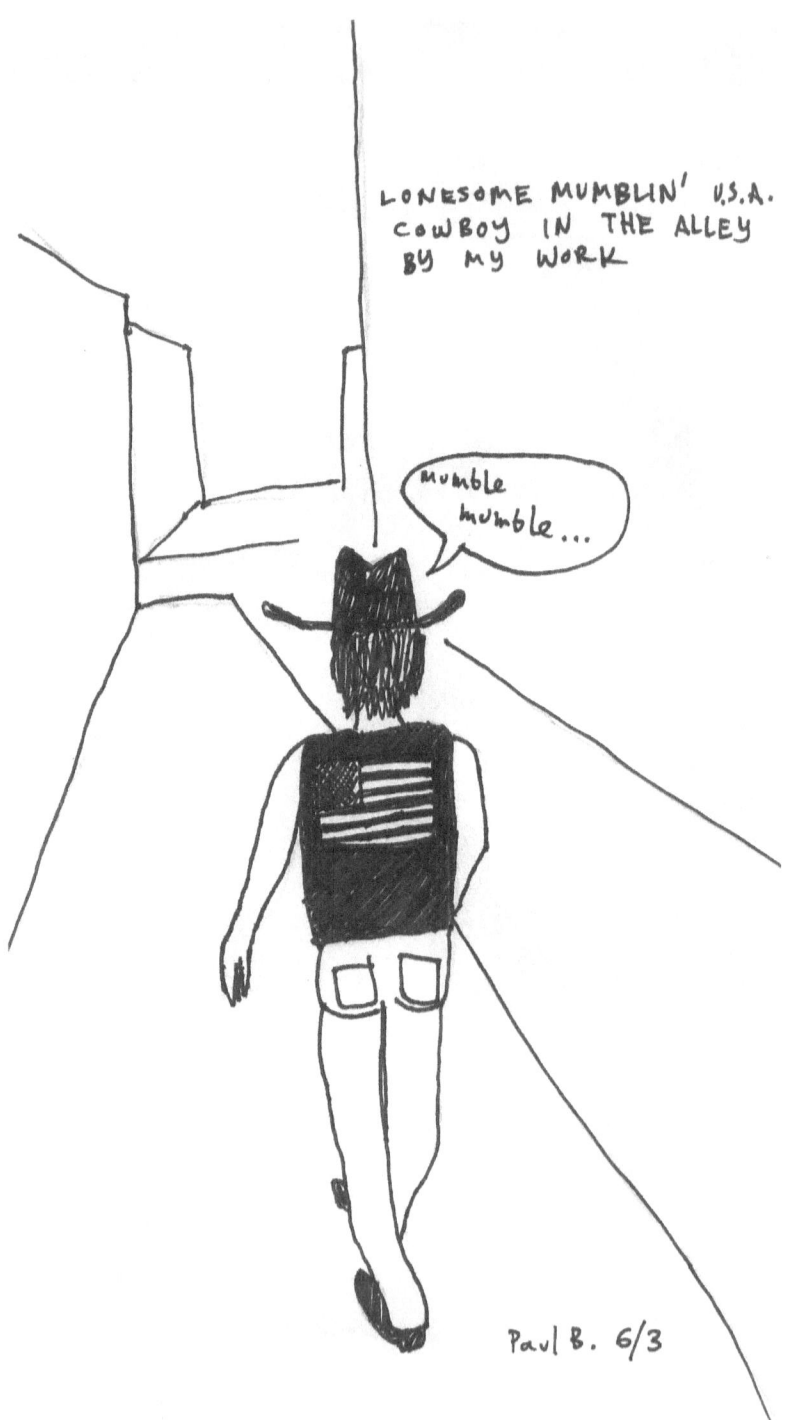

Good advice from a scary bum on a traffic median:

"You want some advice? Da world is fucking shit and people are fucking VACUUMS!!!"

paul
7/15

The Turner kids from down the street in Sonoma. Their druggie parents once fired a gun in the house and would scream at each other and their pack of children constantly. When these awful brats left the house, no small animal was safe.

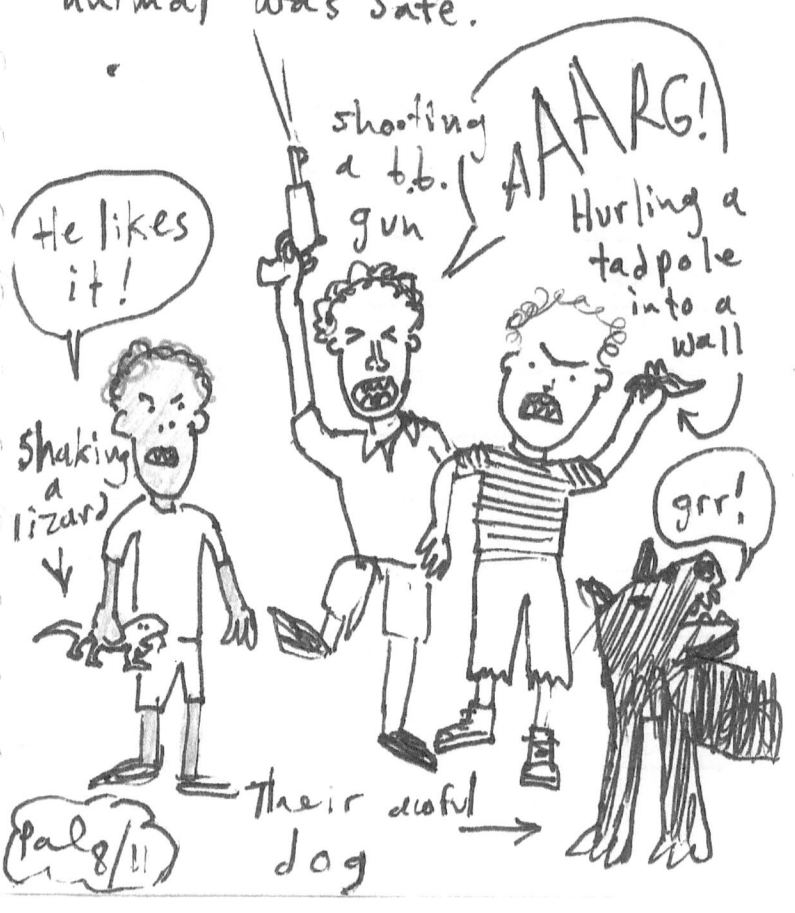

when I broke my arm skating
in a wet drainage ditch, they
gave me a blue and yellow
cast because
I was from
Berkeley.

KISS IT!
WITH Redox
Protectors

I wanted
white.

8/13

Paul

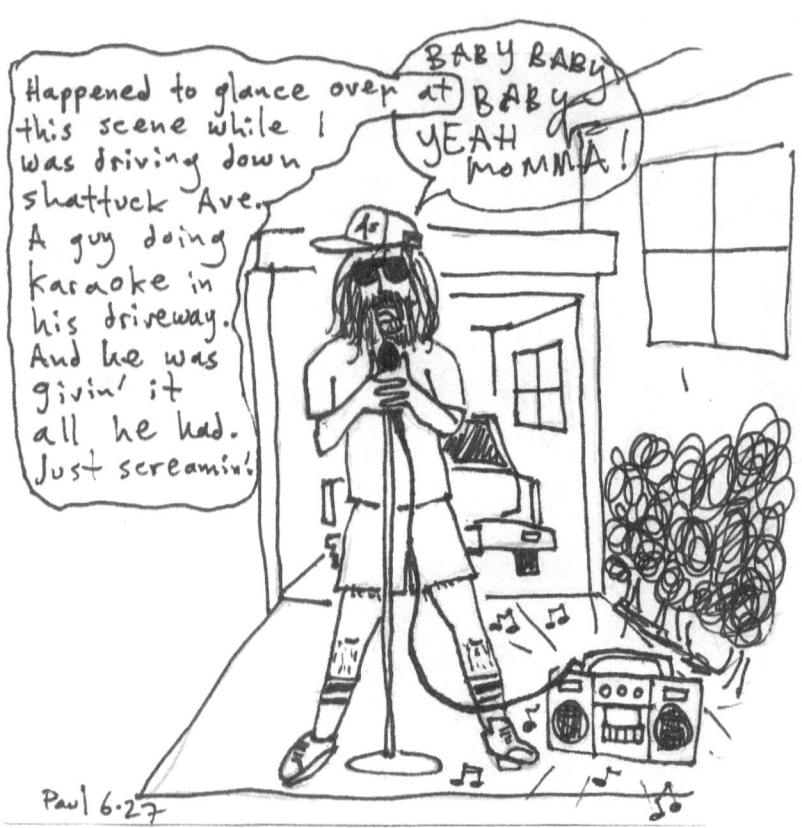

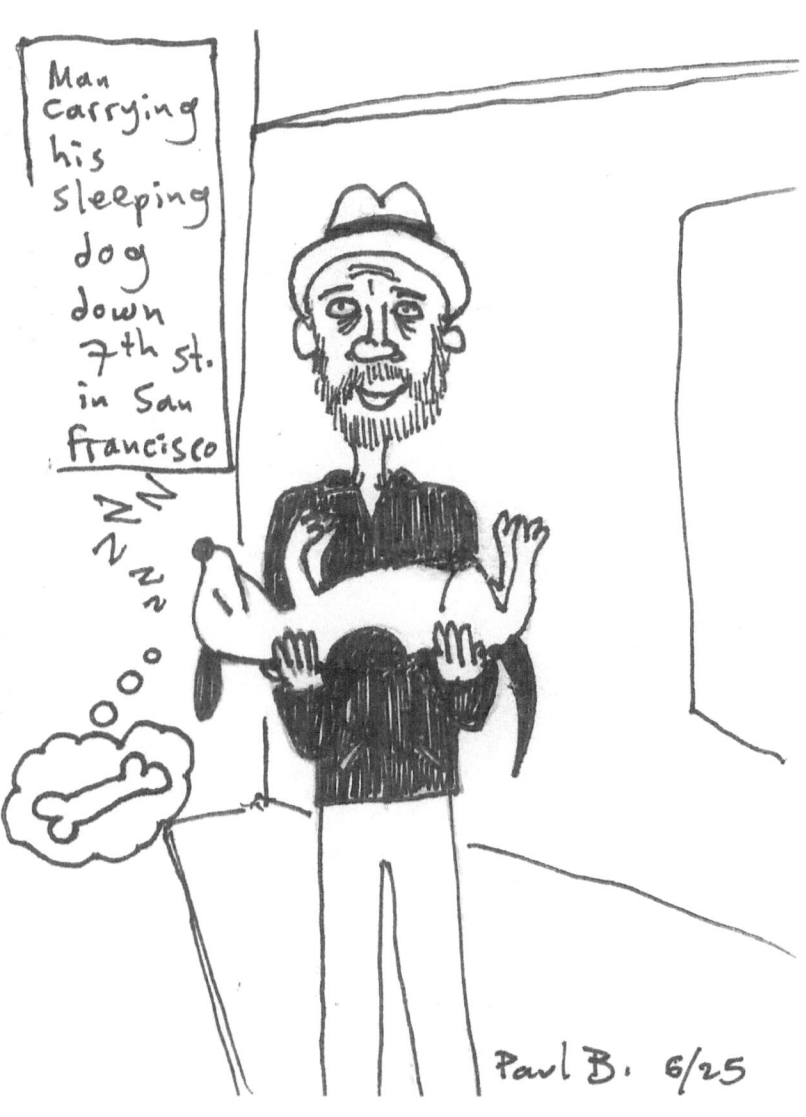

some f\*\*\*ing
bean bag
farted at me
as I walked
behind it
today.

Eff
you,
bean
bag.

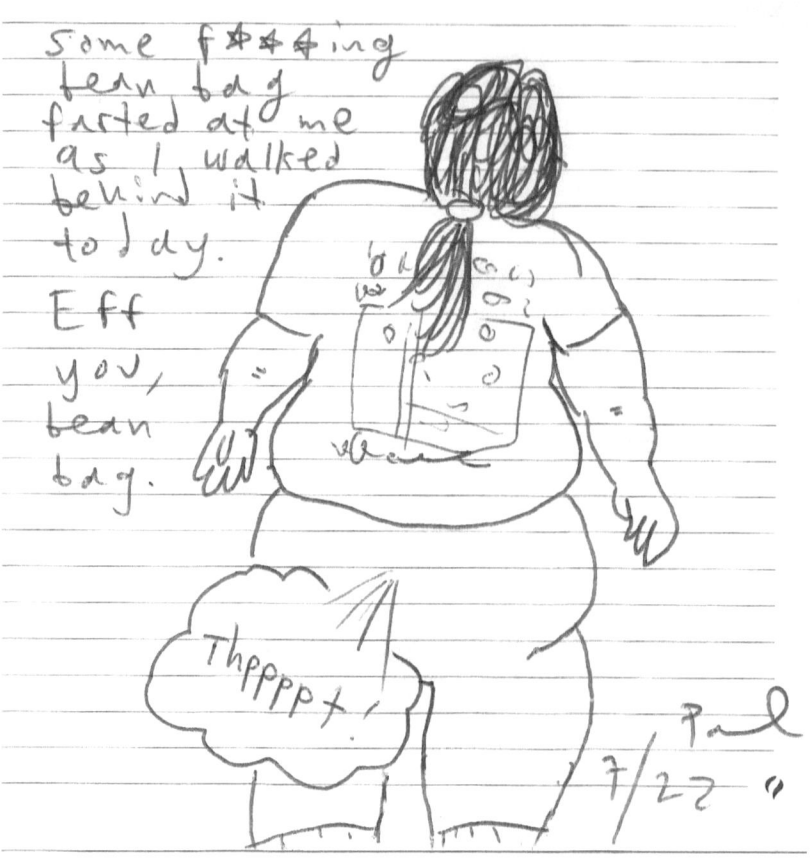

WOMAN
STARING AND
GESTURING
HUNGRILY AT
OUR ~~BEAUTY~~
POT STICKERS
AT SHEN HUA.
THROUGH THE
WINDOW.

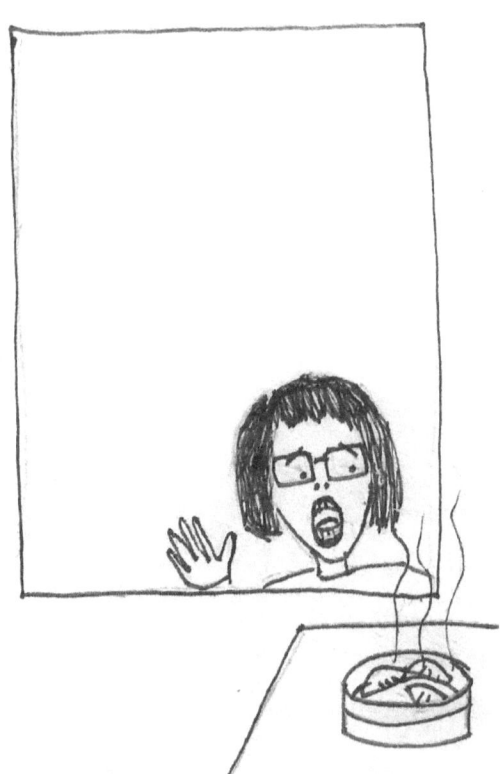

PB 6/19

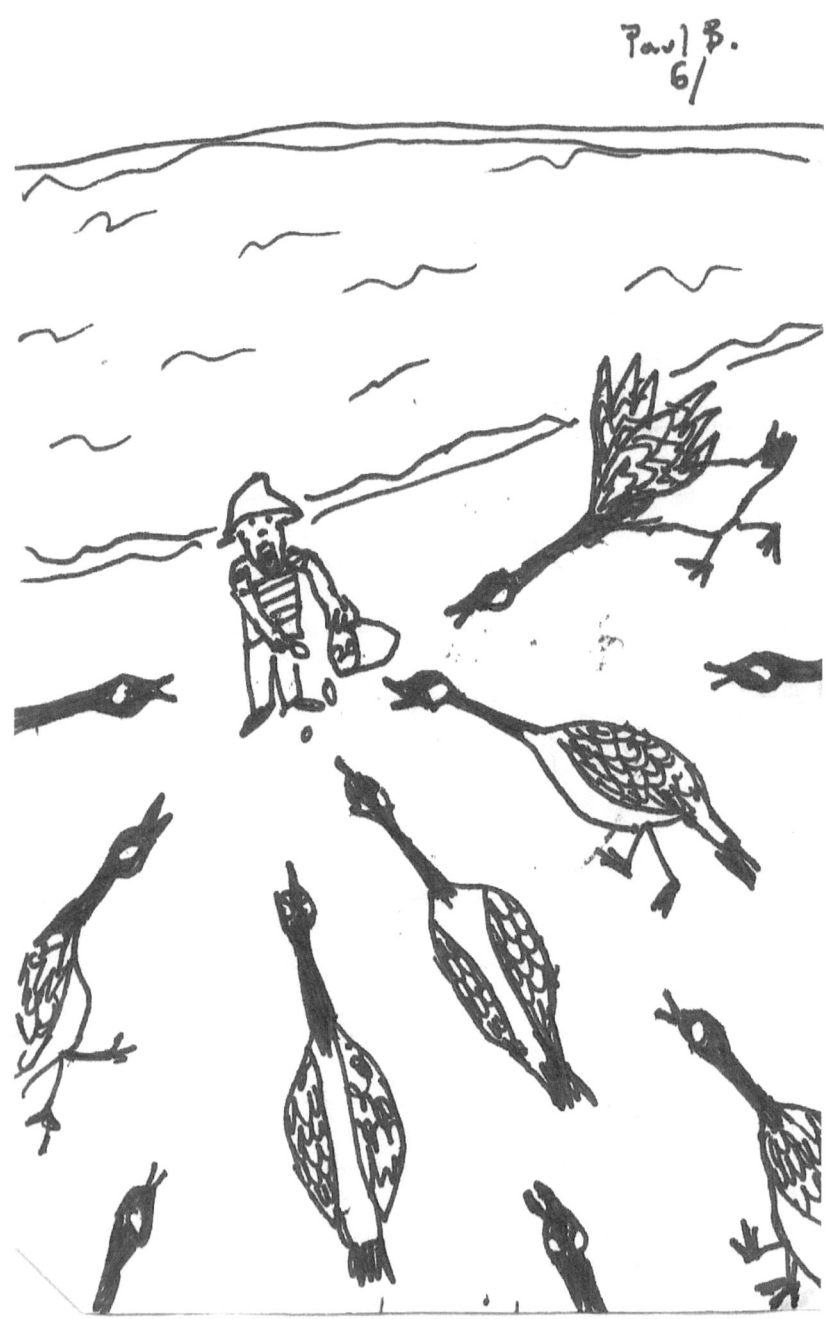

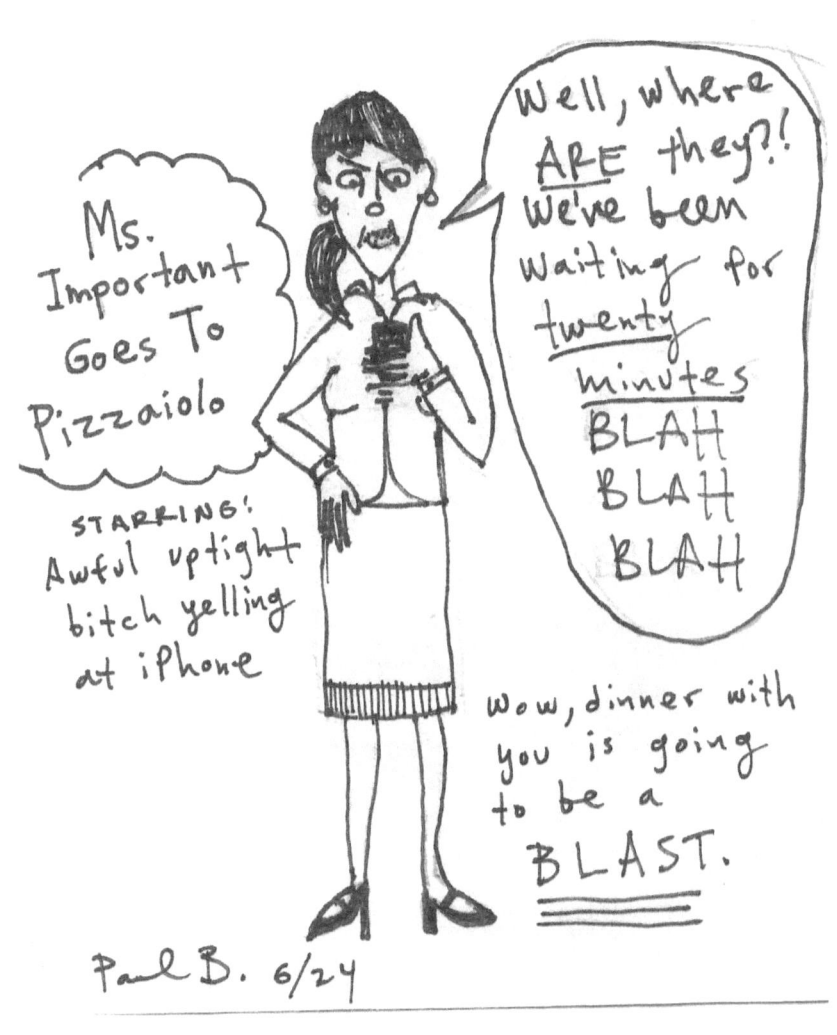

Paul B. 6/24

15

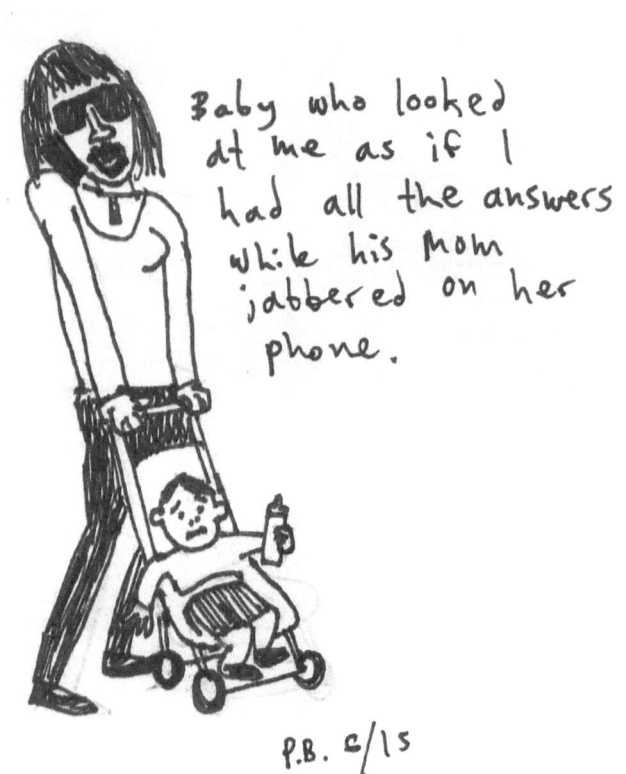

Baby who looked at me as if I had all the answers while his mom jabbered on her phone.

P.B. 6/15

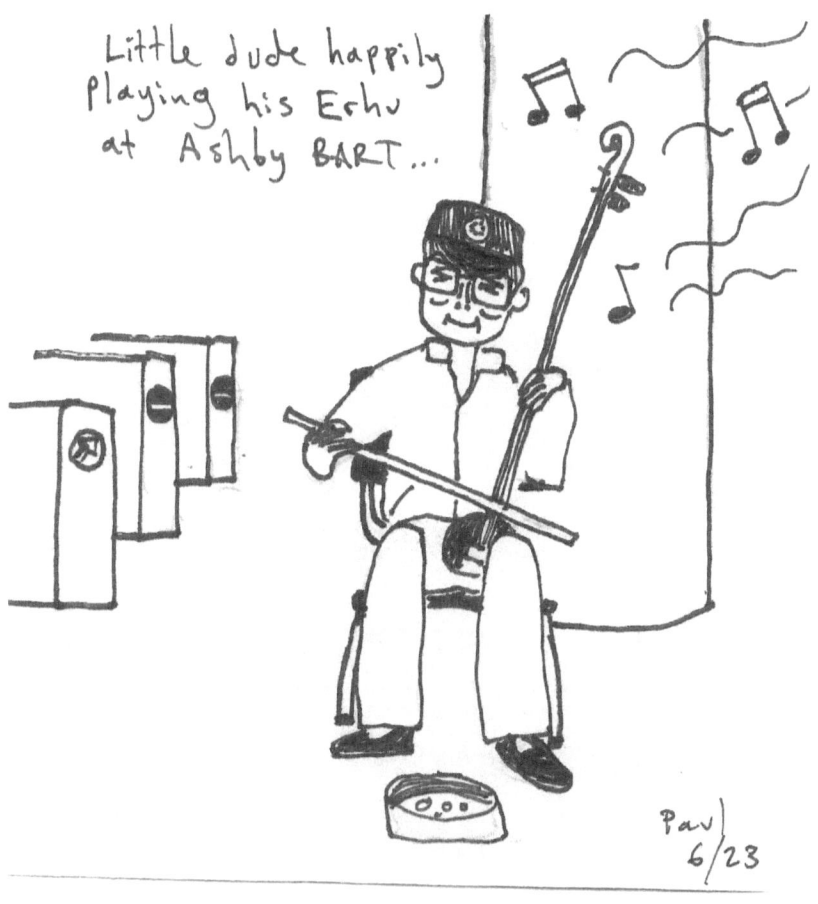

Little dude happily playing his Erhu at Ashby BART...

Pav
6/23

17

Why do fatsies often drive
aggressively and tailgate?

Because the automobile is
the one place in society
in which the playing field
is level. The only place where
they have equal social power.
Plus, they are probably hella

hungry.

Paul 7/25

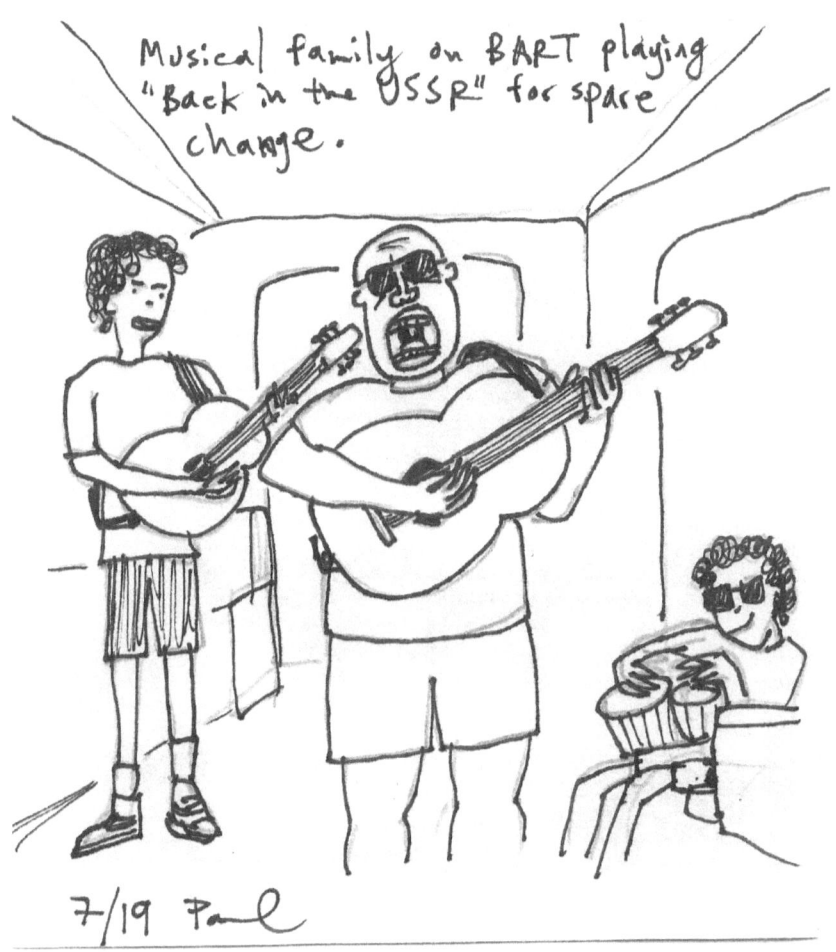

Musical family on BART playing "Back in the USSR" for spare change.

7/19 Paul

Let's go to a
restaurant and
fiddle with our iPhones
together.

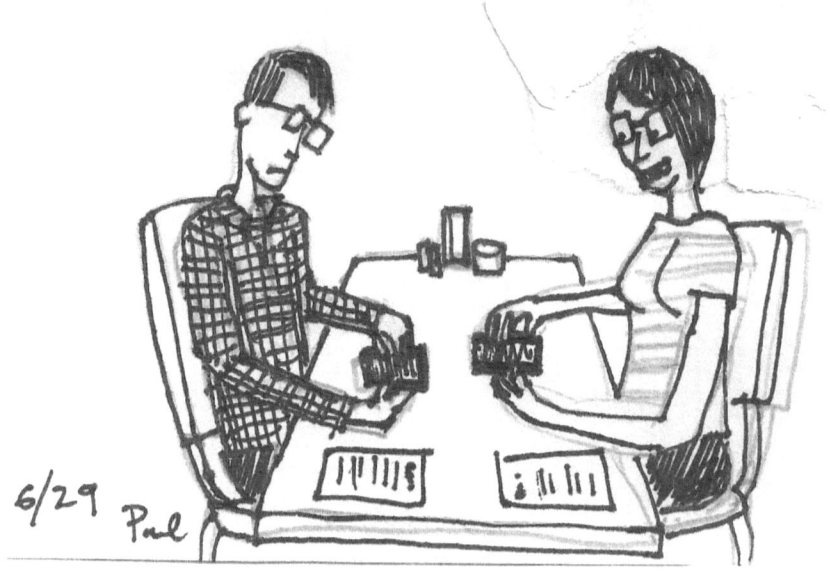

6/29 Paul

As if riding a
Unicycle in a non-
circus situation
doesn't make you
enough of a
dickhead.

Nope, you had to
take it one step
further and add
the ice cream
cone.

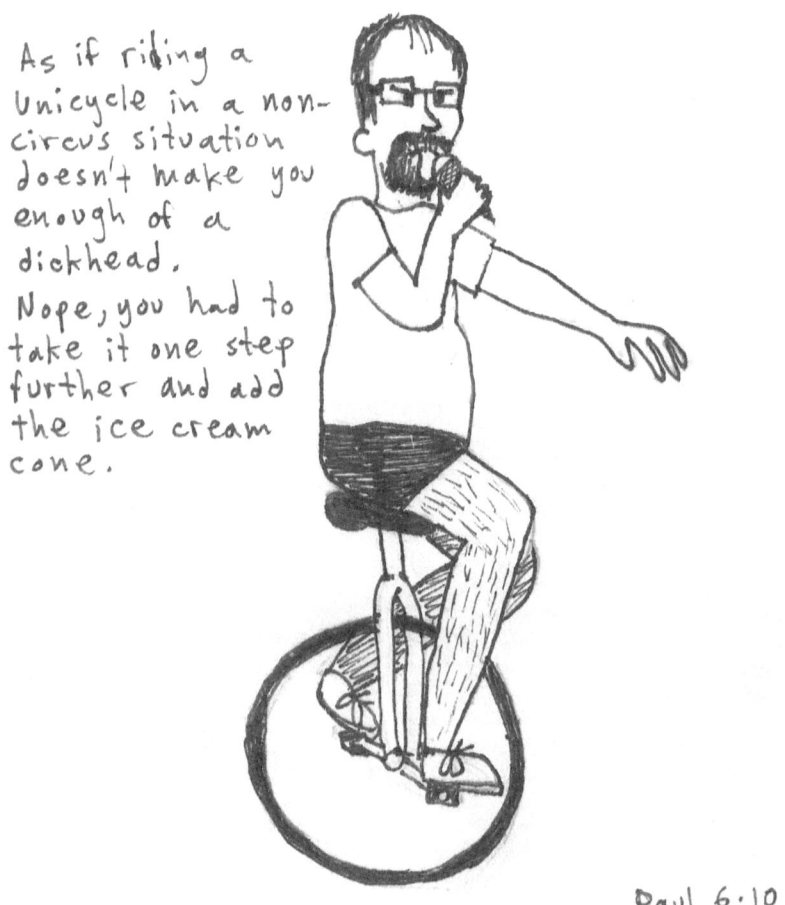

Paul 6·10

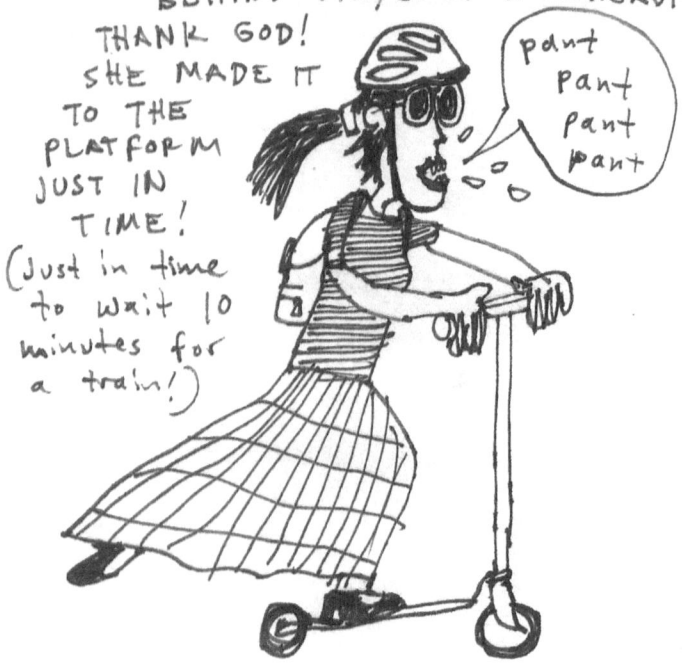

RUSHING THROUGH THE BART STATION ON HER LITTLE SCOOTER, THEN RUNNING DOWN THE STAIRS BEHIND ME, BREATHING HEAVILY.

THANK GOD! SHE MADE IT TO THE PLATFORM JUST IN TIME! (Just in time to wait 10 minutes for a train!)

Paul 6/14

22

MORE STARBUCKS FUN!!!

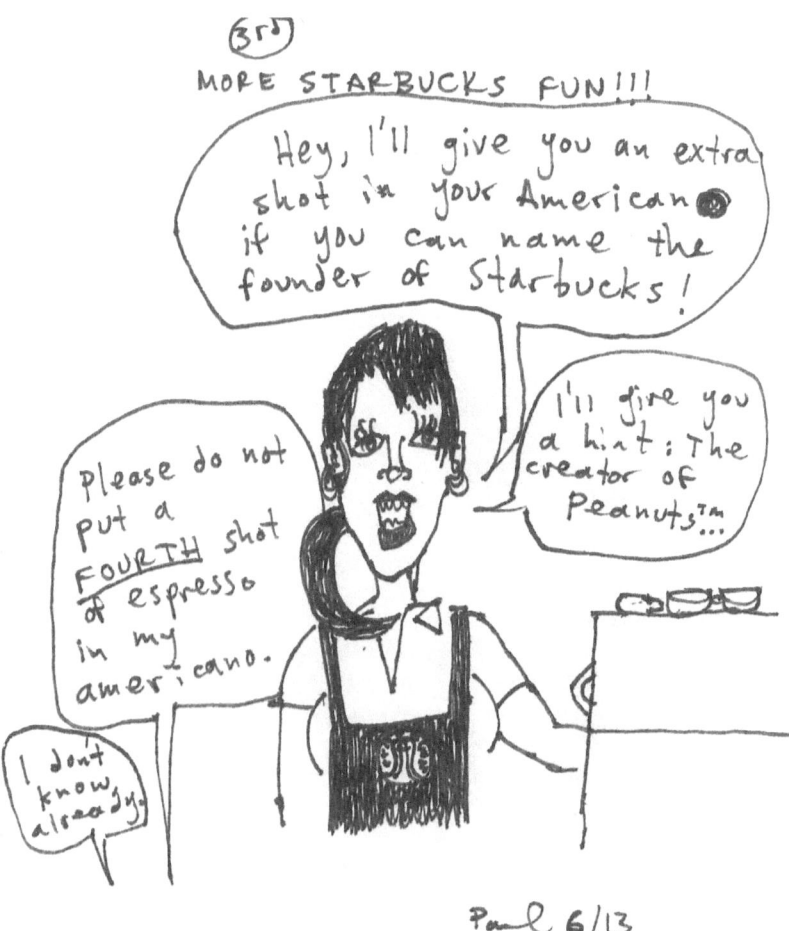

Paul 6/13

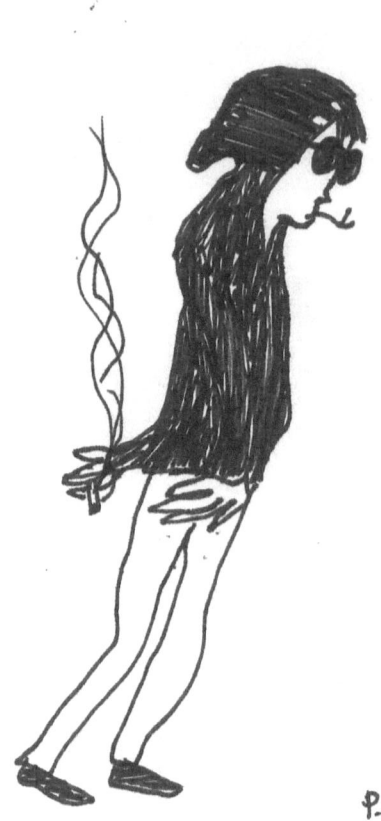

saw this
junkie-snake
type person
today on Russ
and Folsom.
I added the
forked tongue
for snake
emphasis.

P.B. 6/16

chubby ~~little~~, boyish-looking adult man
with Prince Valiant haircut
yelling into cellphone in Bart station.

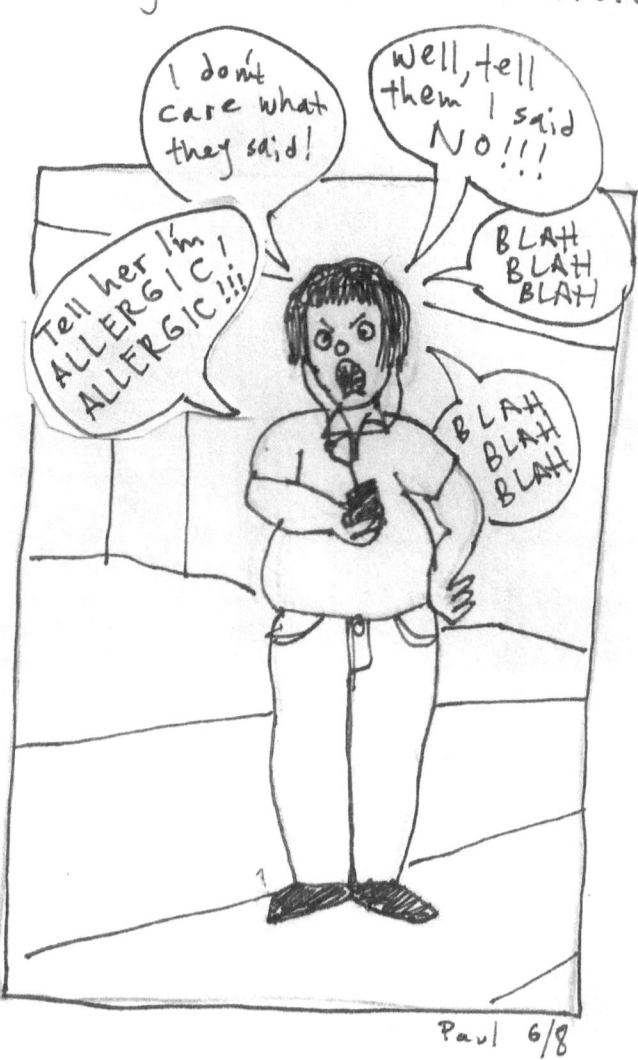

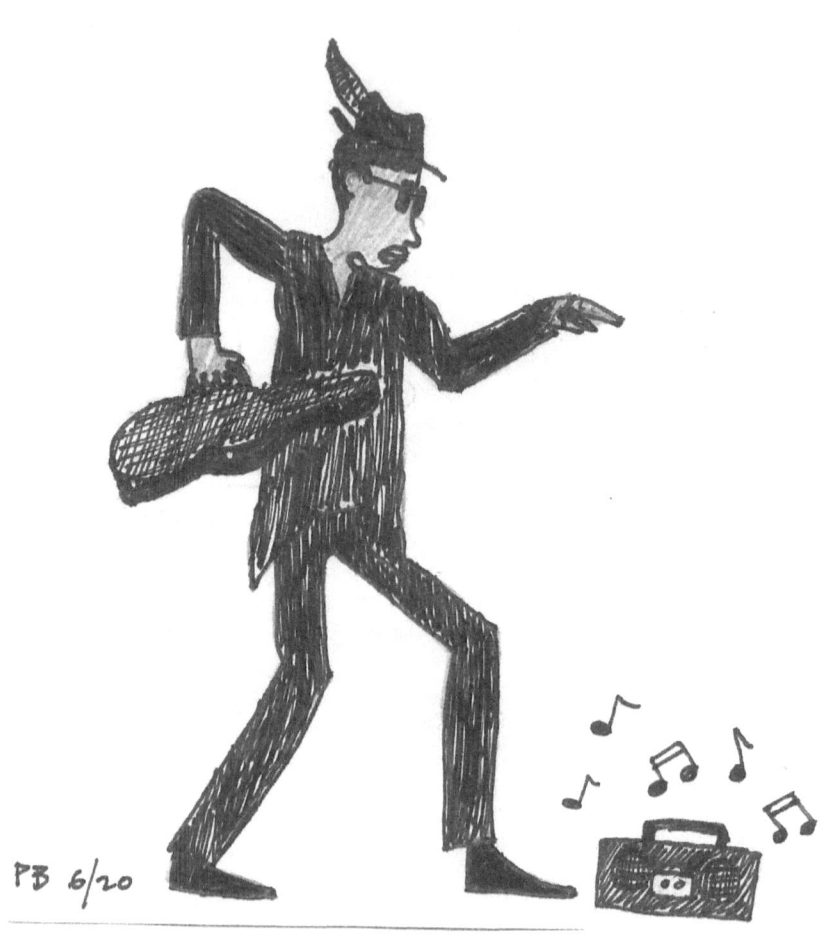

PB 6/20

26

COUPLE WHO WERE ALMOST HIT BY
A GREEDY MOTORIST IN A CROSSWALK
NEAR THE NEW TRADER JOE'S ON UNIV.

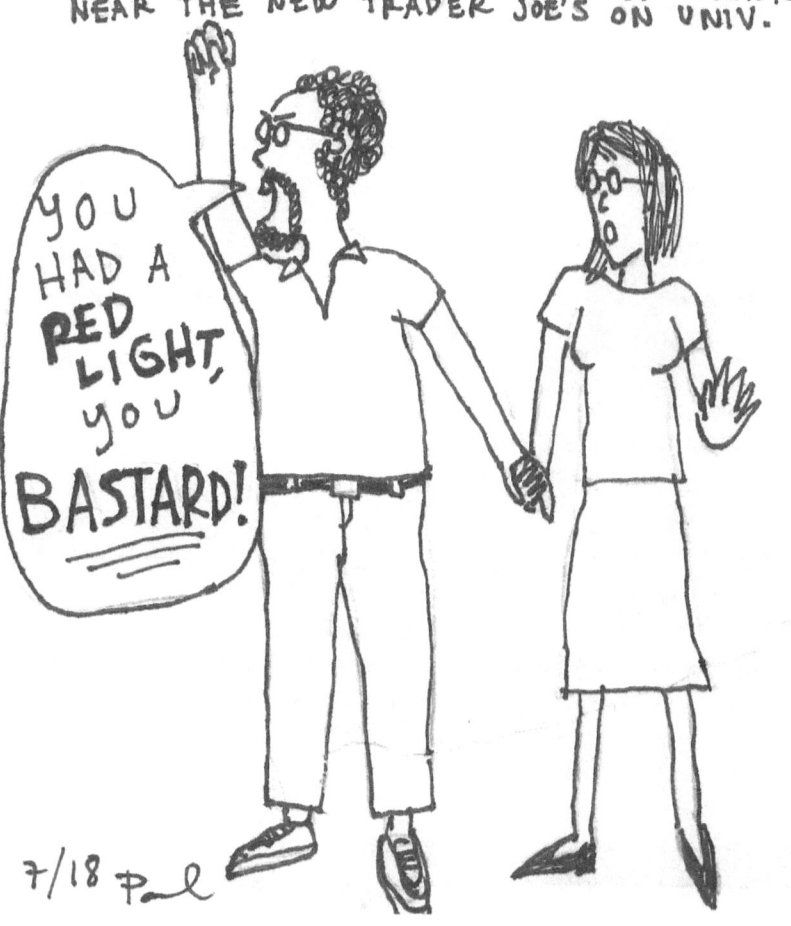

These two guys stopped for a rest in front of the coffee rostery where I work. One was relaxing on a t.v. he had been transporting while the other beat out a rhythm on his legs.
They were both drunk, it was around 11:15 a.m.

Paul
6·17

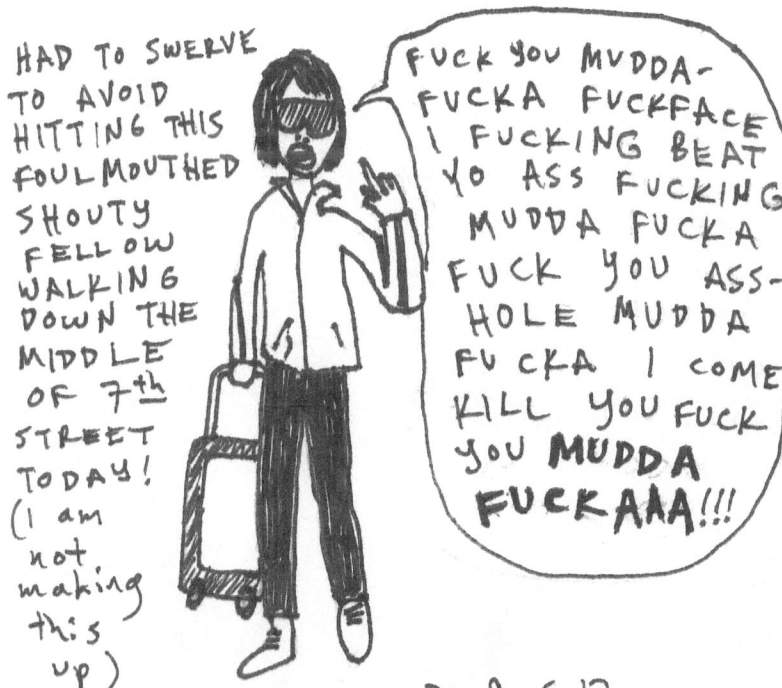

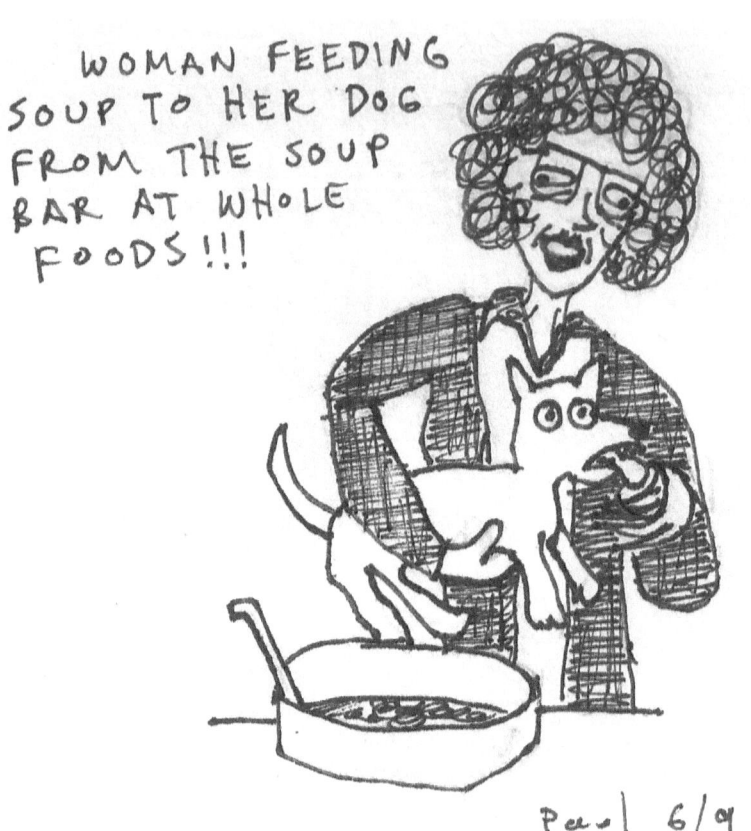

WOMAN FEEDING
SOUP TO HER DOG
FROM THE SOUP
BAR AT WHOLE
FOODS!!!

Paul 6/9

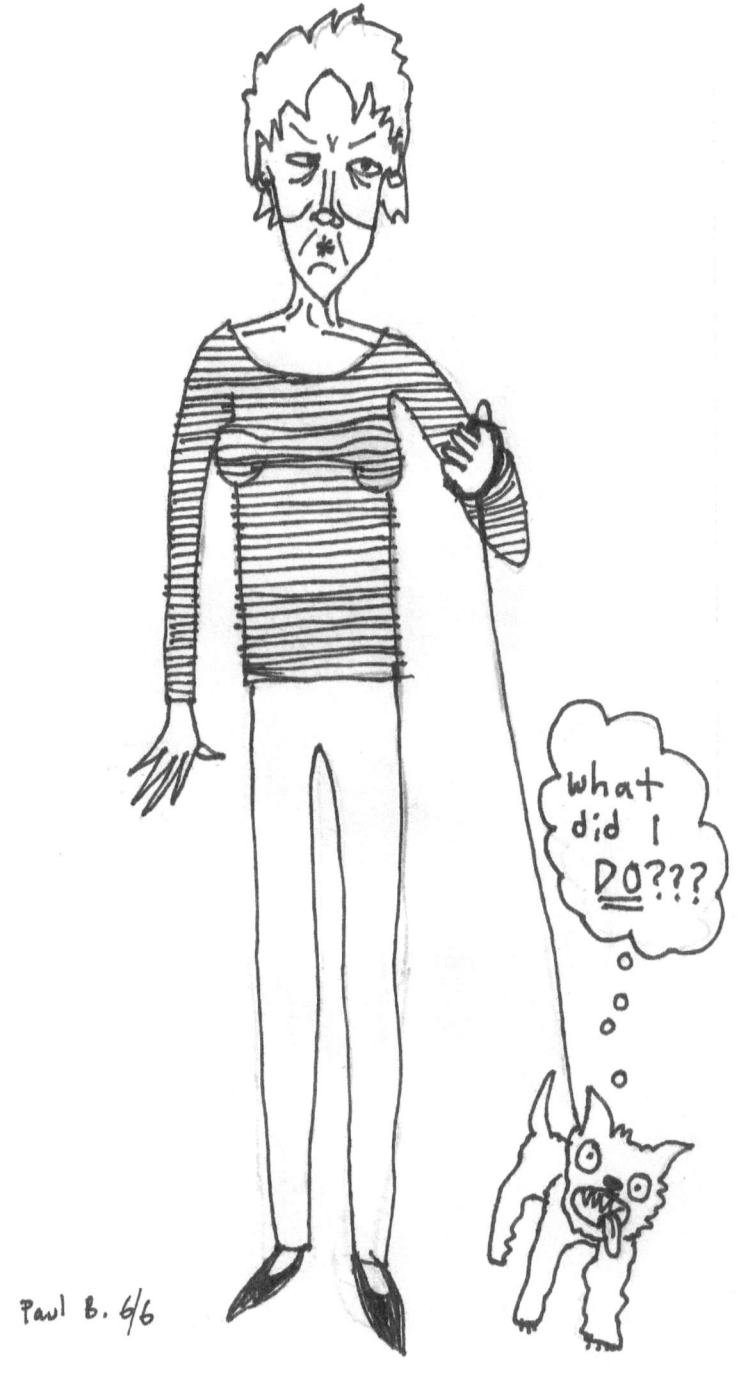

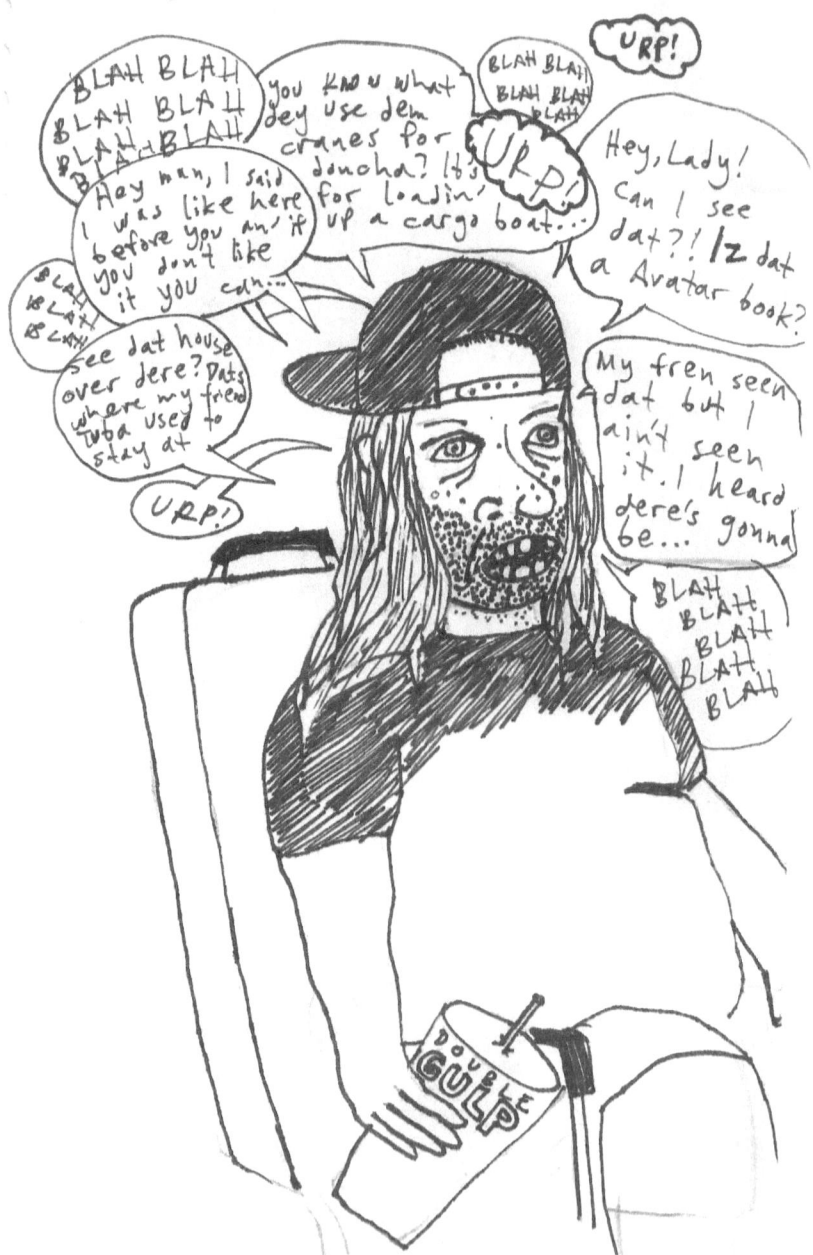

LOVE IS A MANY-SPLENDORED THING

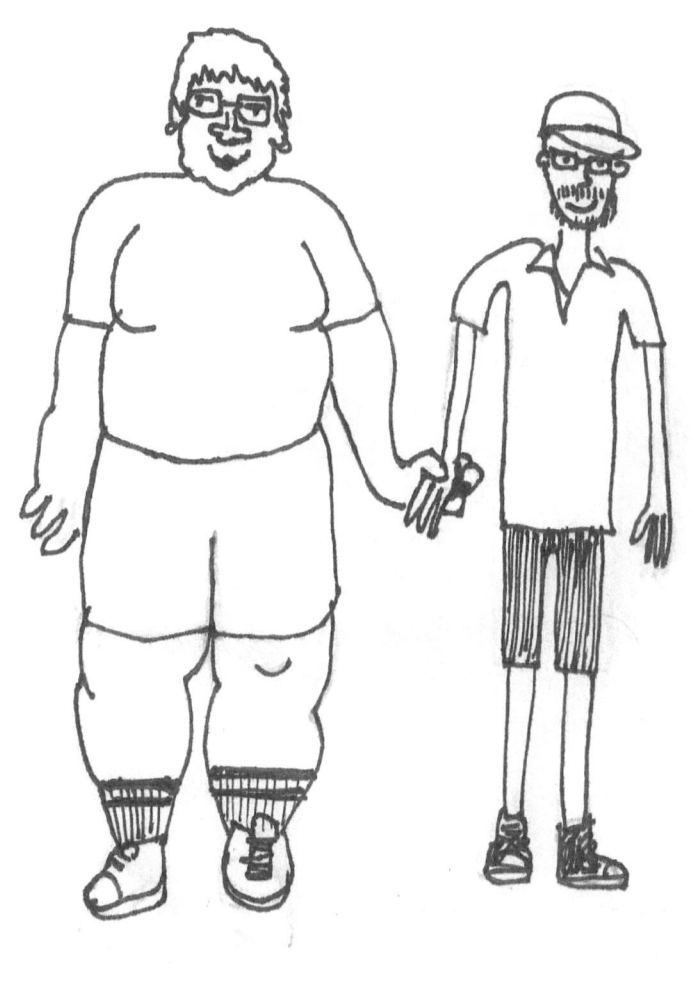

c/s Paul

# MISSION CREEK 2

## ATTACK OF THE CLONES

Denim Jacket    wayfarers

Blossom Hat

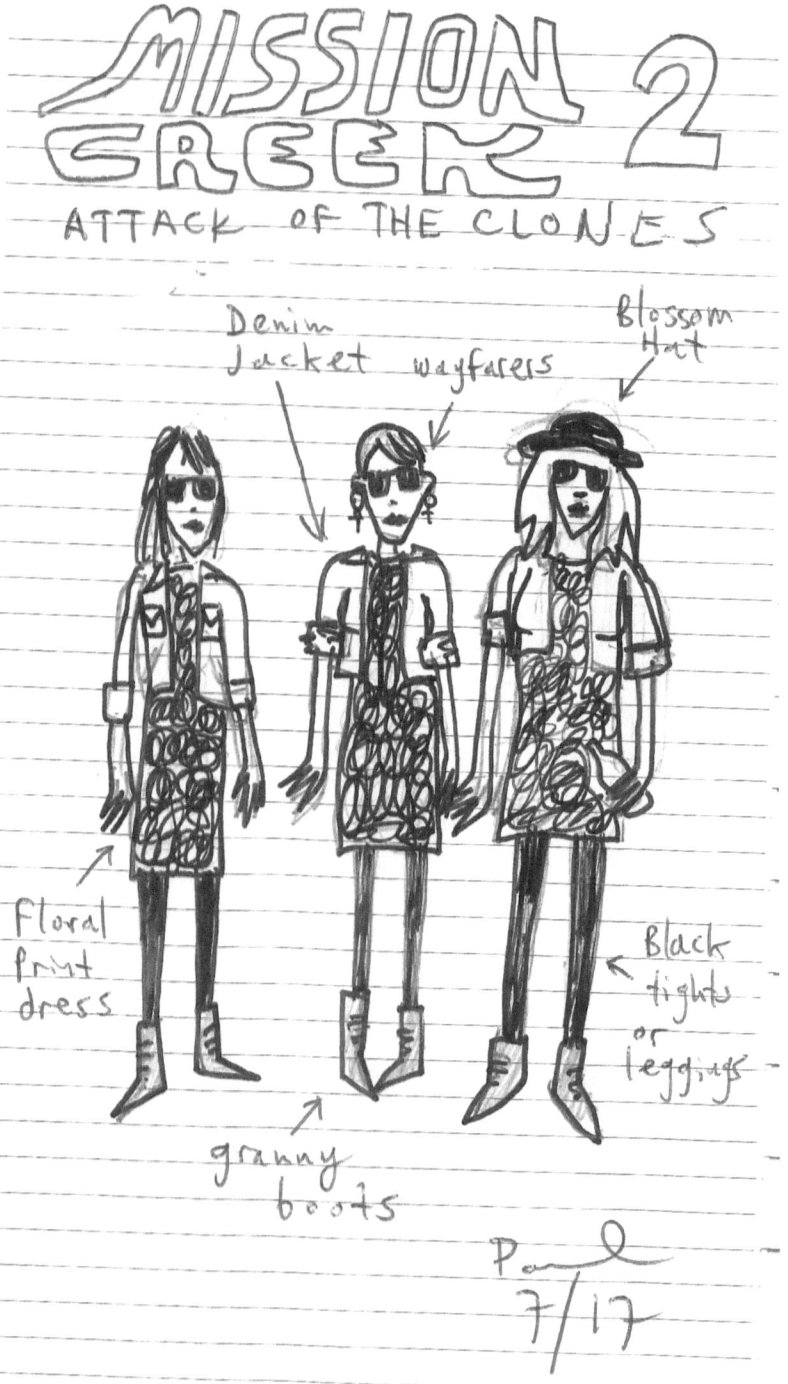

Floral
Print
dress

Black
tights
or
leggings

granny
boots

Paul
7/17

Guy with dyed-green
mustache and
propeller bike
helmet riding
down Woolsey.
Whatever.

Paul
2/27

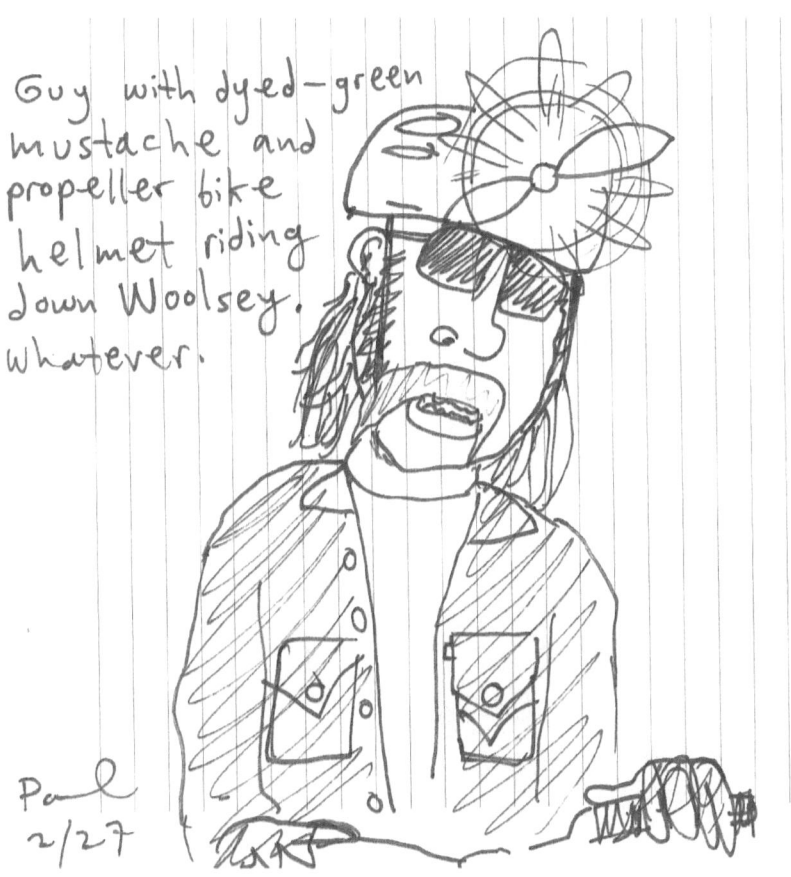

Spotted this albino dude wearing camo and a "utility kilt". For some reason he was chewing on a big cigar stub.
At first I was happy to have found my P.O.T.W. for the day, but then I high-tailed it outta there before he let off the nerve gas or threw a Molotov cocktail.

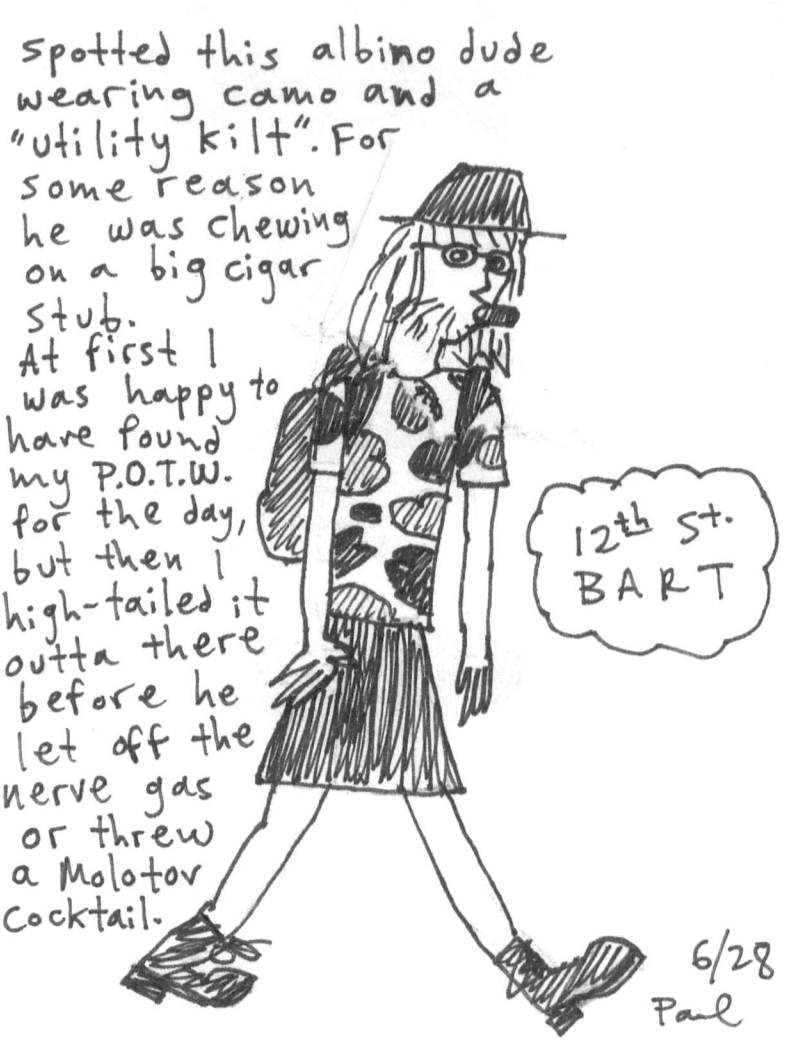

12th St. BART

6/28
Paul

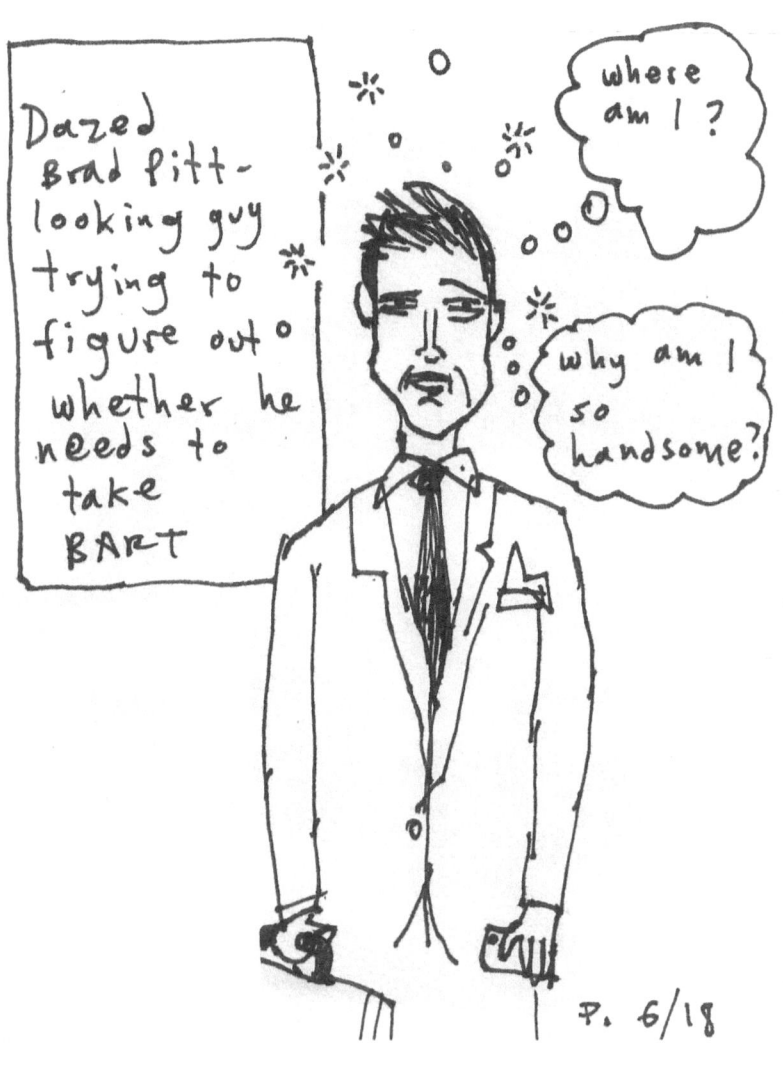

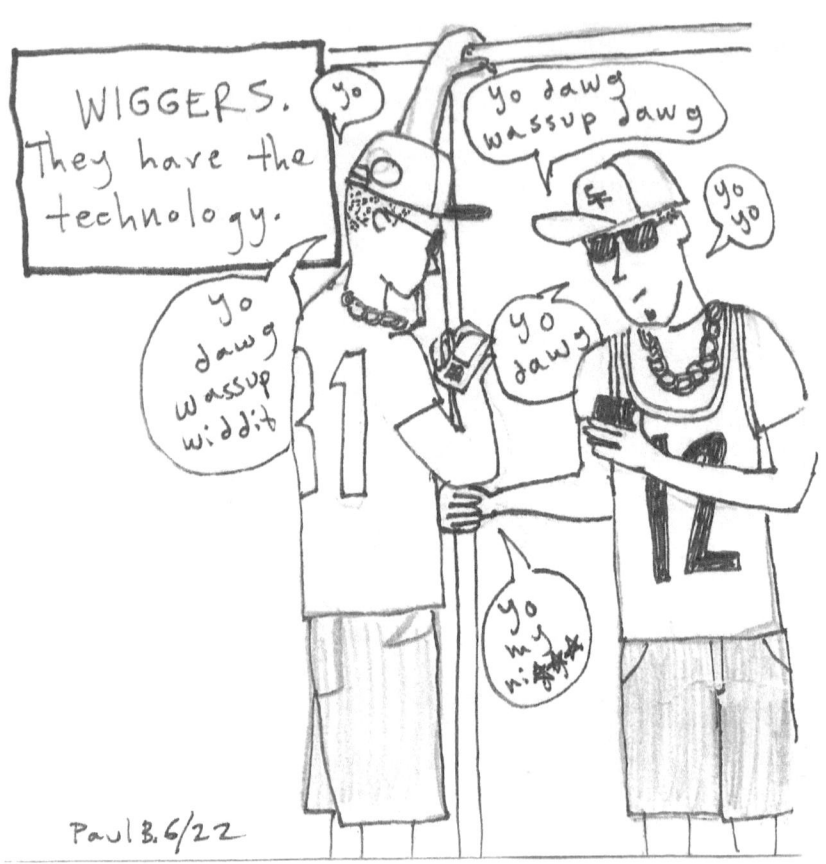

Paul B. 6/22

38

Dude on a bicycle that was
also a motorcycle or something.

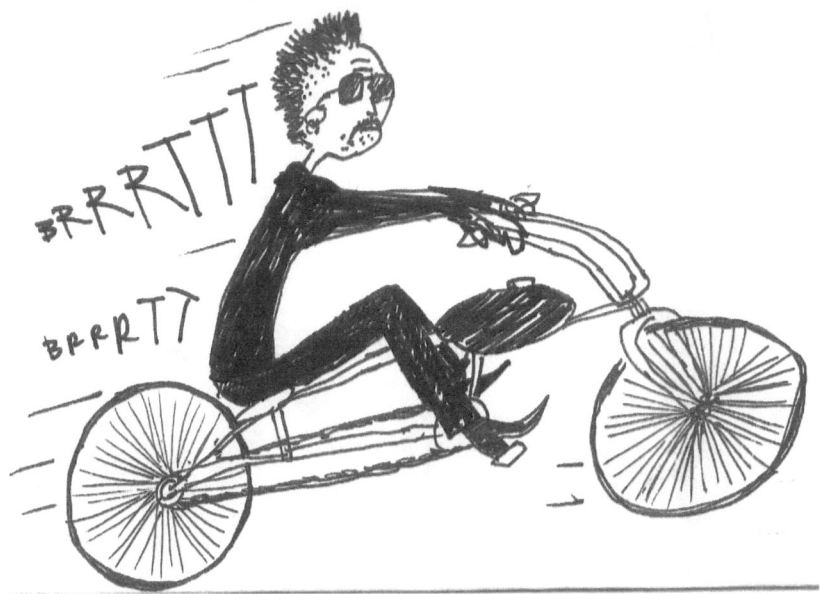

This neurotic babbler standing in line at Trails Cafe boring everyone within earshot with her verbal diarrhea MUST be from Berkeley.

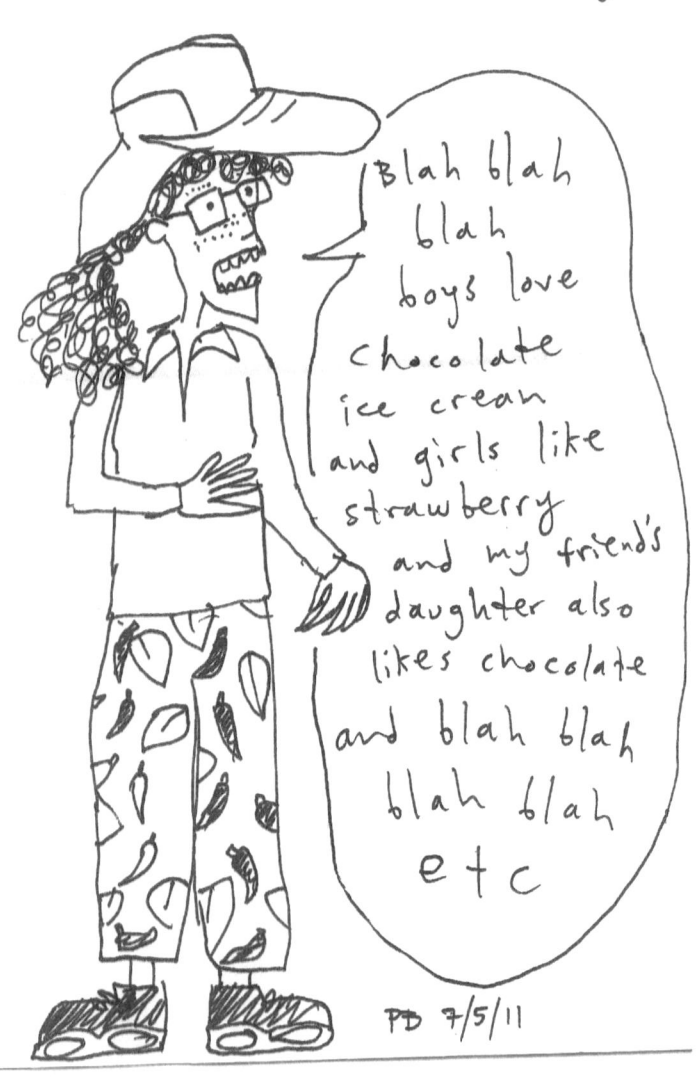

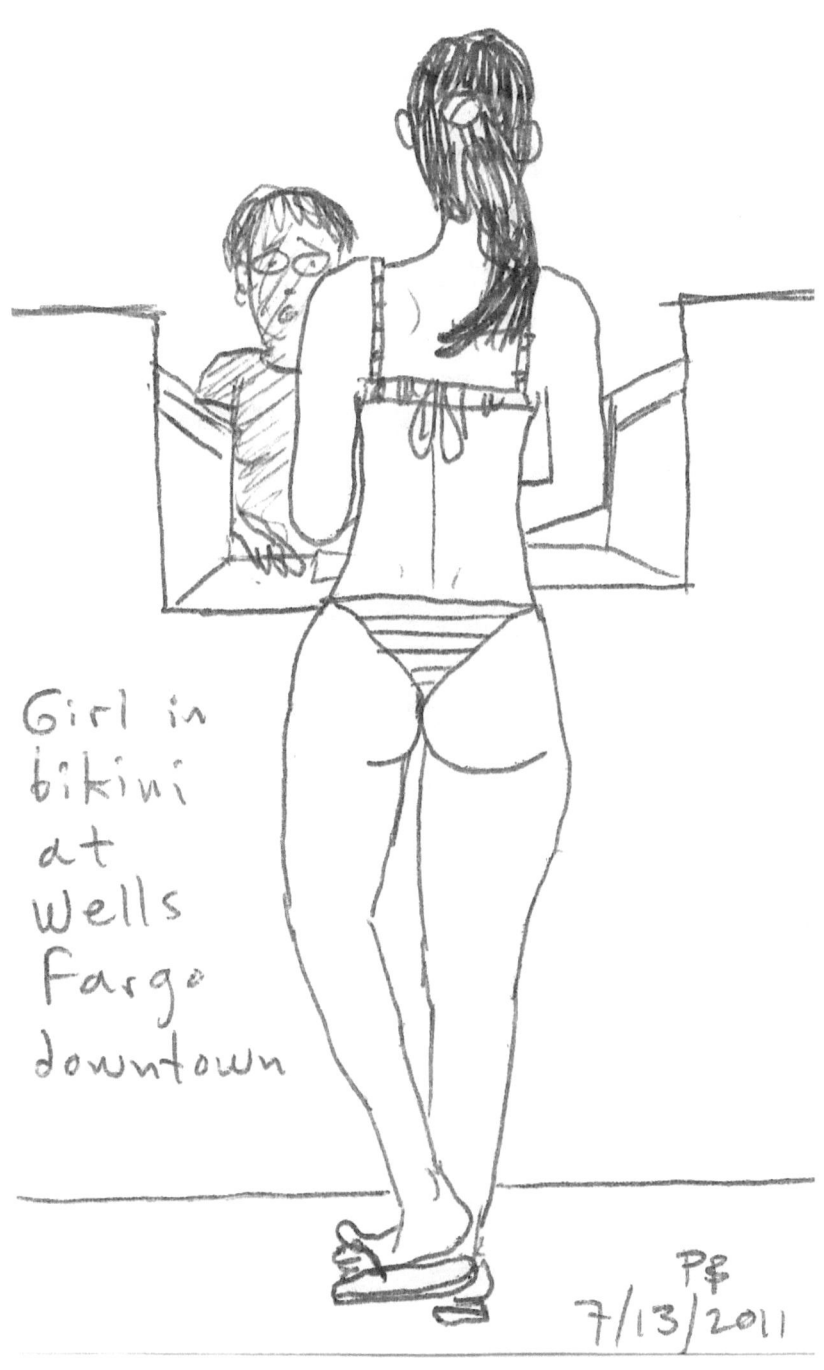

Girl in
bikini
at
Wells
Fargo
downtown

P$
7/13/2011

Johnny Ray —
The punk/new wave kid I
wanted to be like
in
Middle
School

Did you guys tape the punk show on KPFA last night? I did, and you cant borrow it.

Raul 8/04

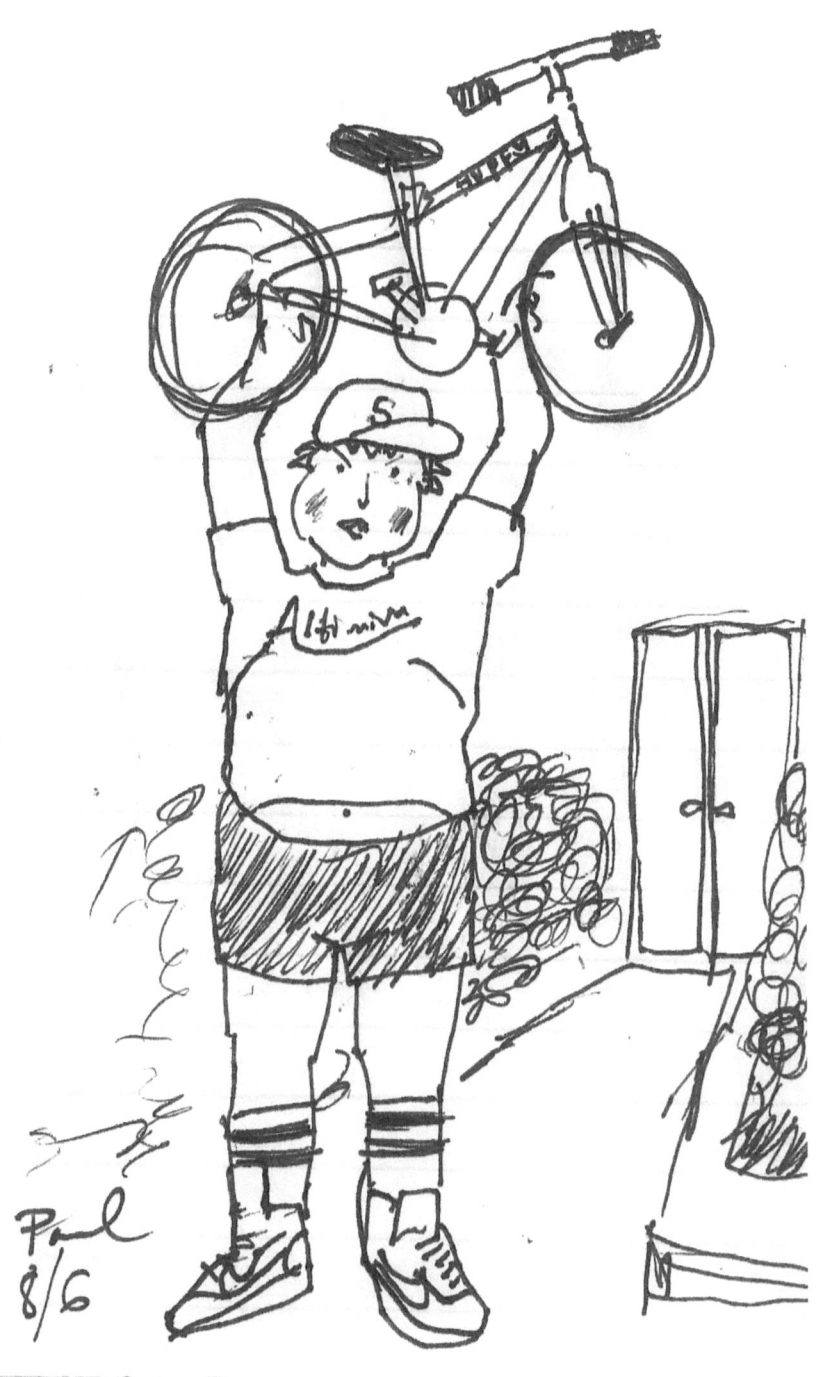

Guy raps over beat on phone while other guy in pilgrim hat and huge jeans dances. In front of pot Distribution place.

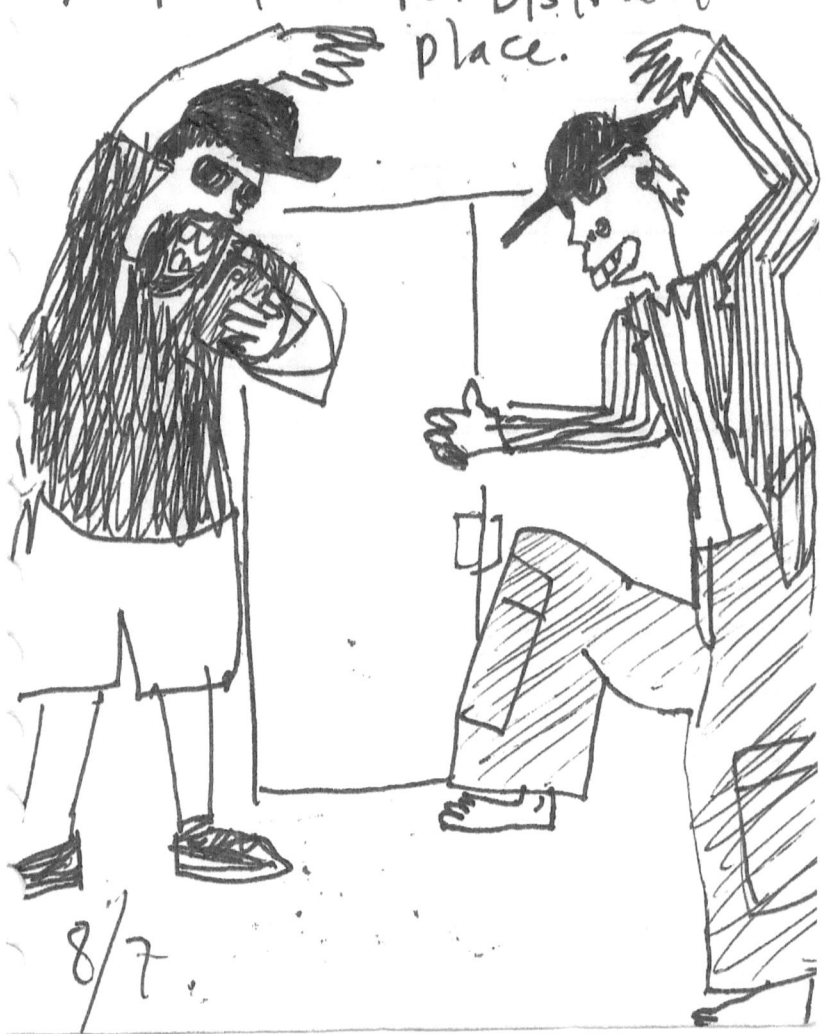

8/7.

Drunk
homeless
fellow
having
a delight-
ful
time

painting
his nails
bright pink.

Folsom
&
Russ
streets in
SOMA

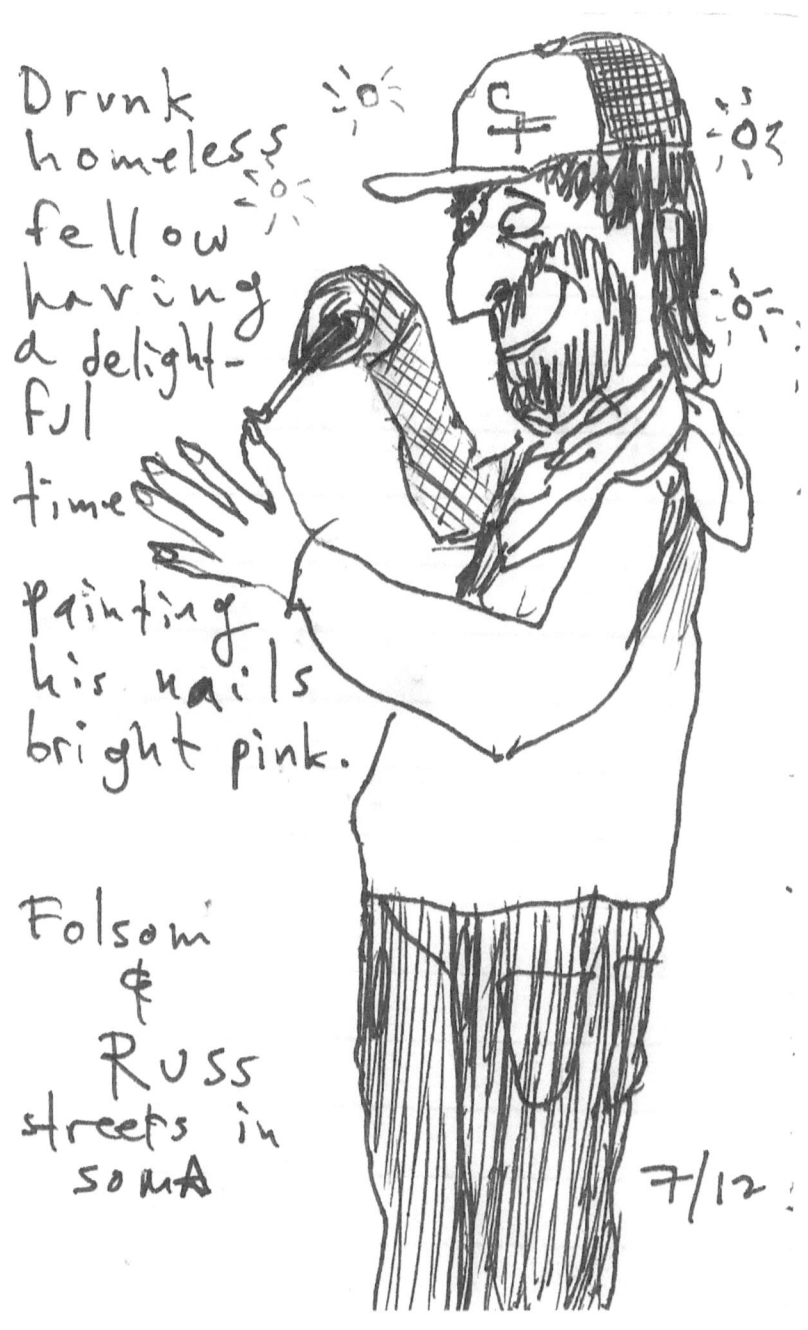

7/12:

45

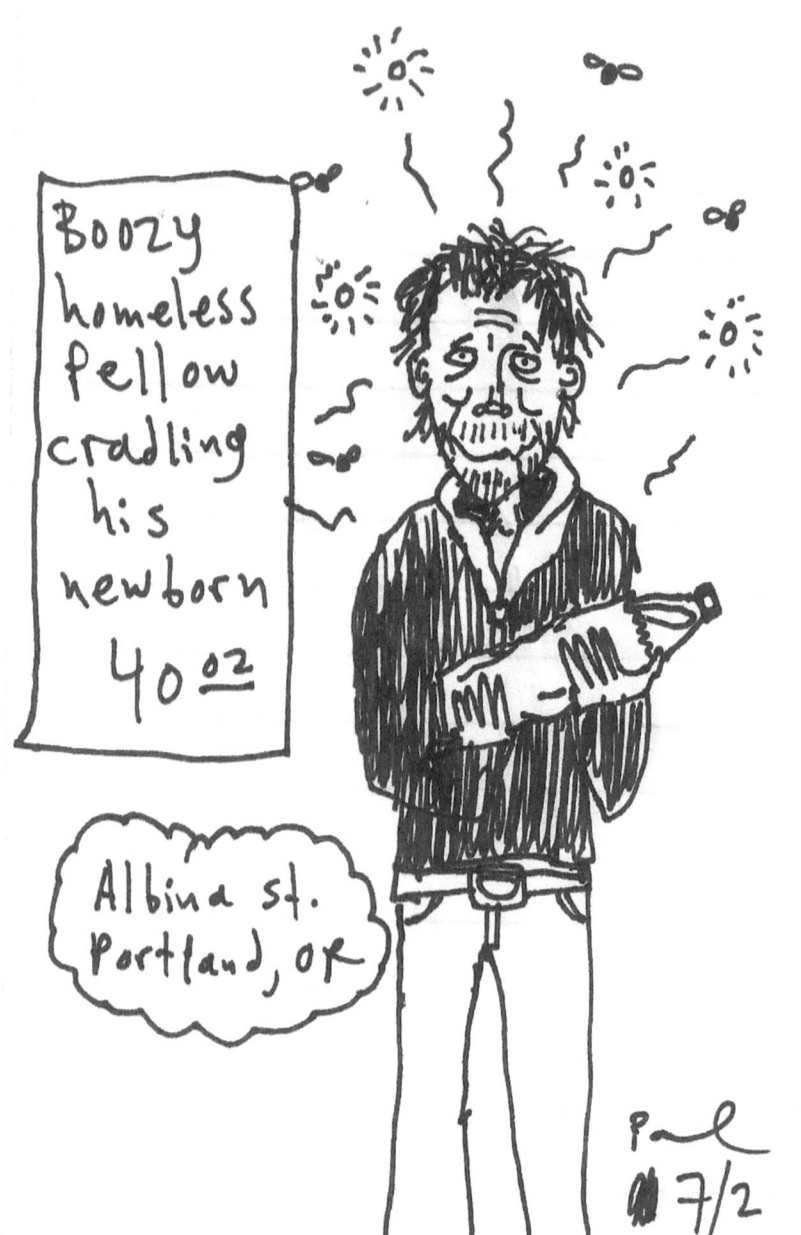

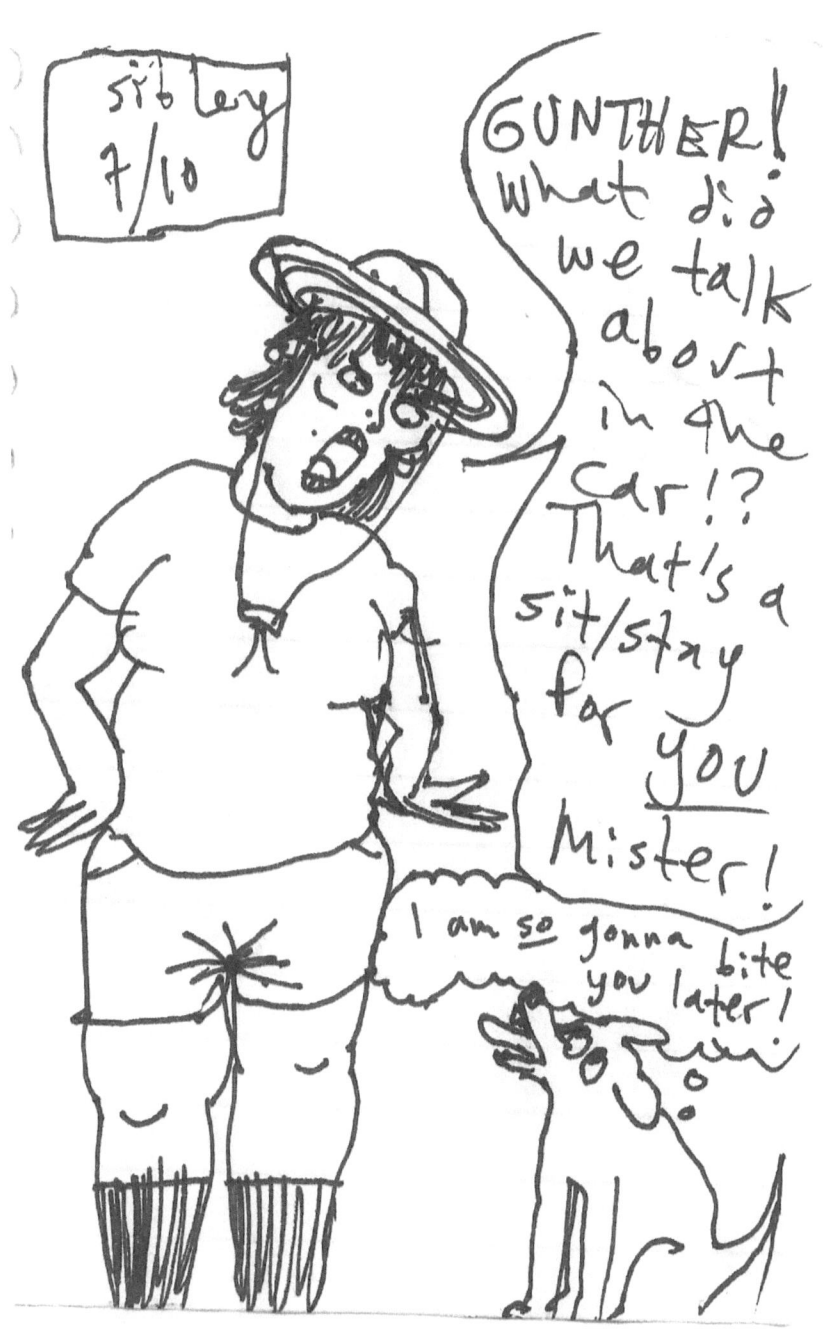

Guy with "Livestrong" visor grooving to his iPod while standing in "power stance" on BART. Those Oakley blades don't make you invisible, dude. I can SEE you.

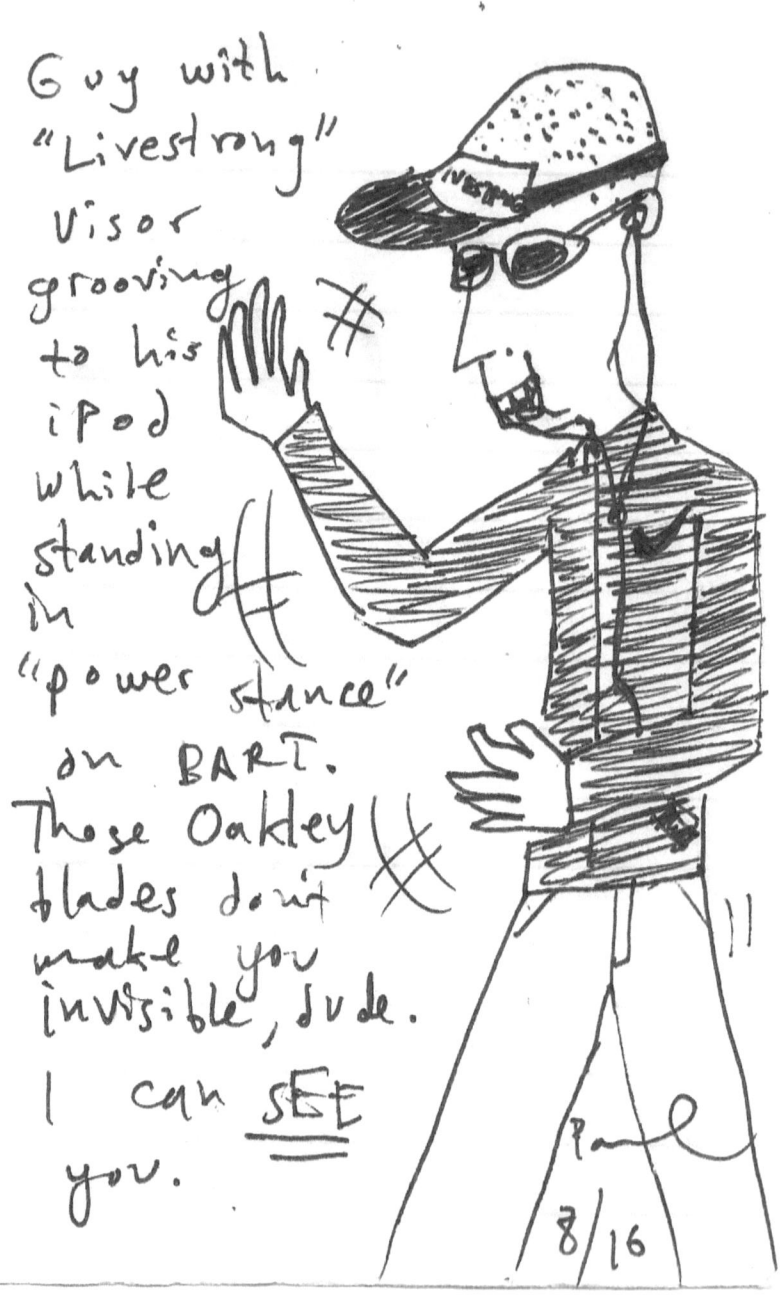

Paul
8/16

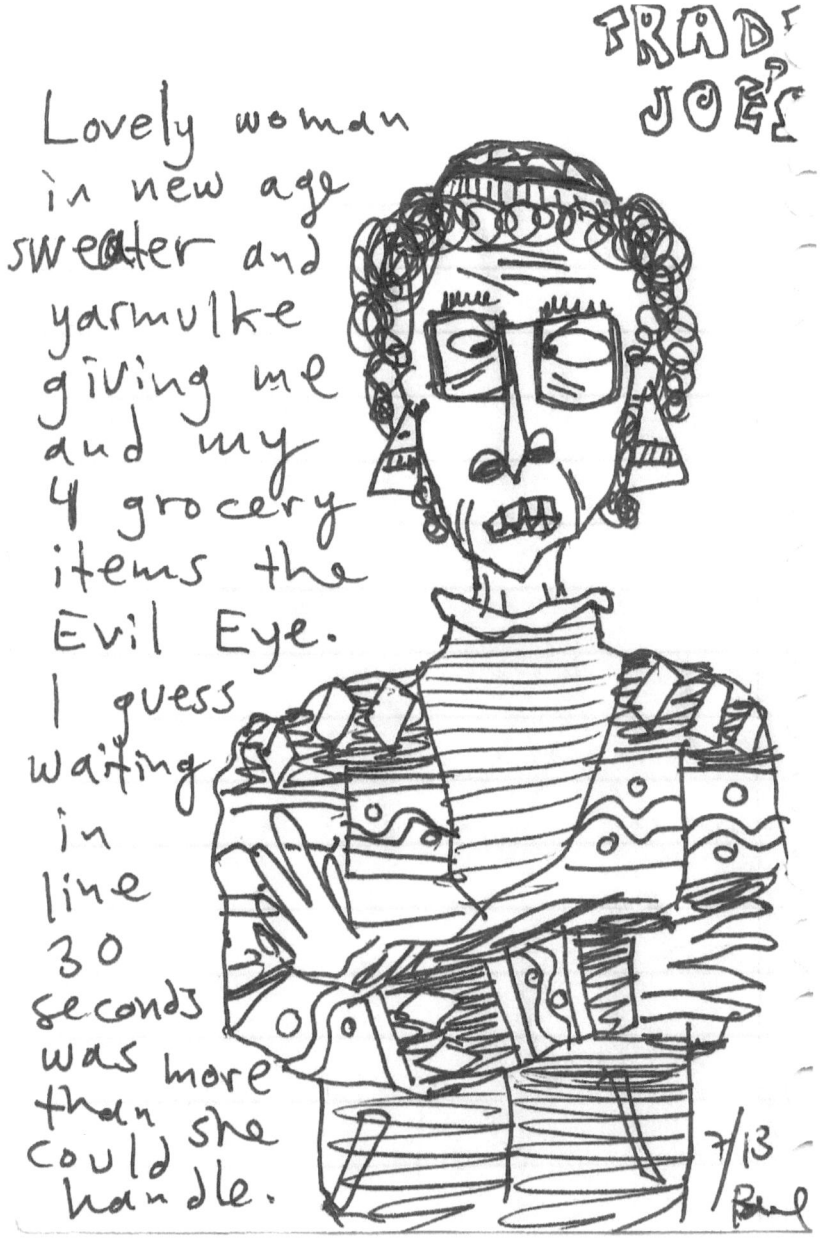

Lovely woman in new age sweater and yarmulke giving me and my 4 grocery items the Evil Eye. I guess waiting in line 30 seconds was more than she could handle.

TRADER JOE'S

7/13
Bond

49

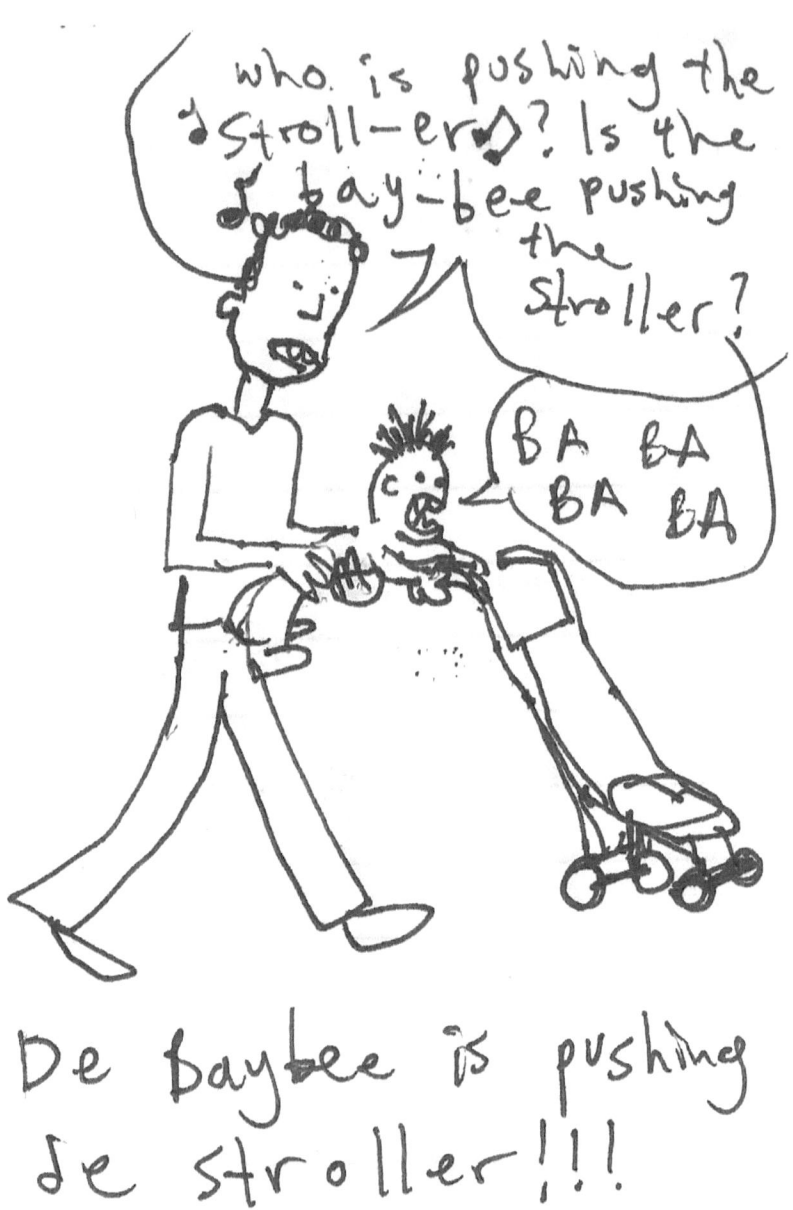

De baybee is pushing
de stroller!!!

6/30

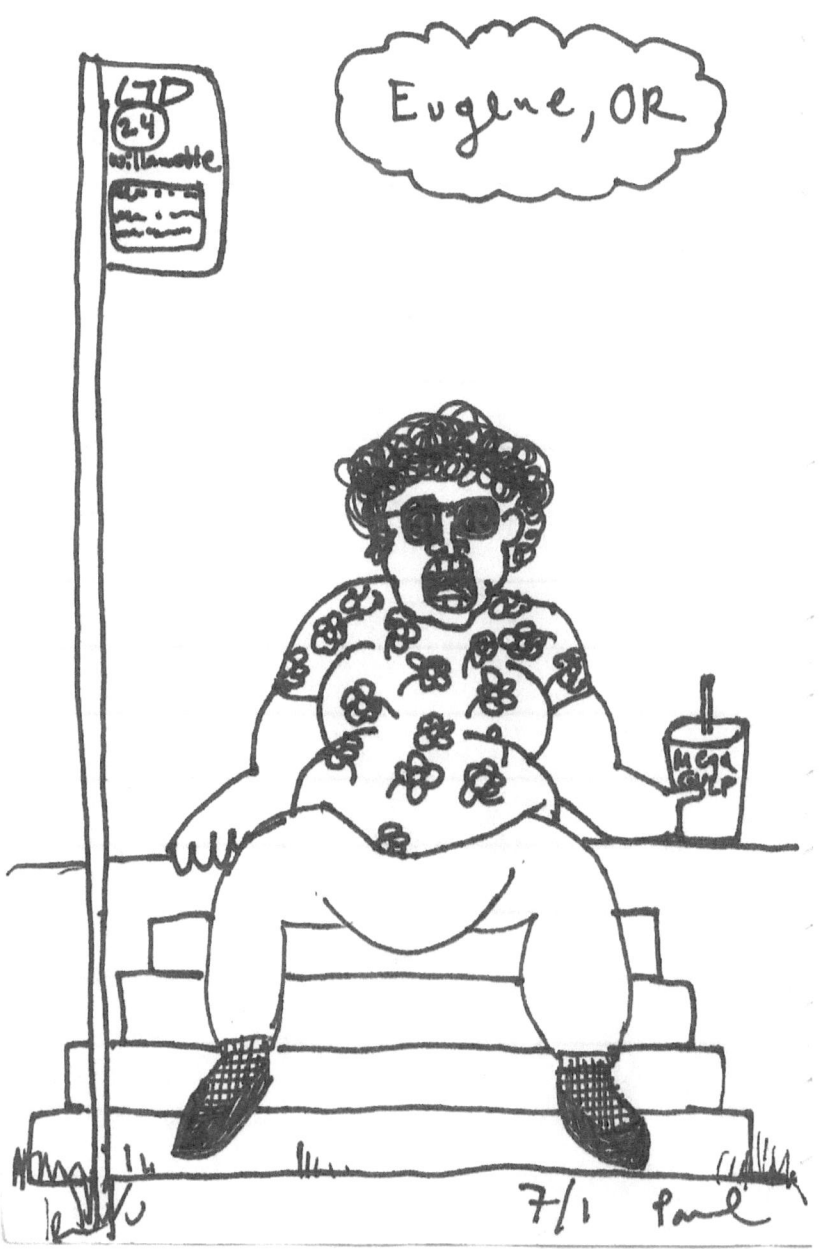

51

Tough lookin'
brother with
cyclops
sunglasses.

The
T.L.

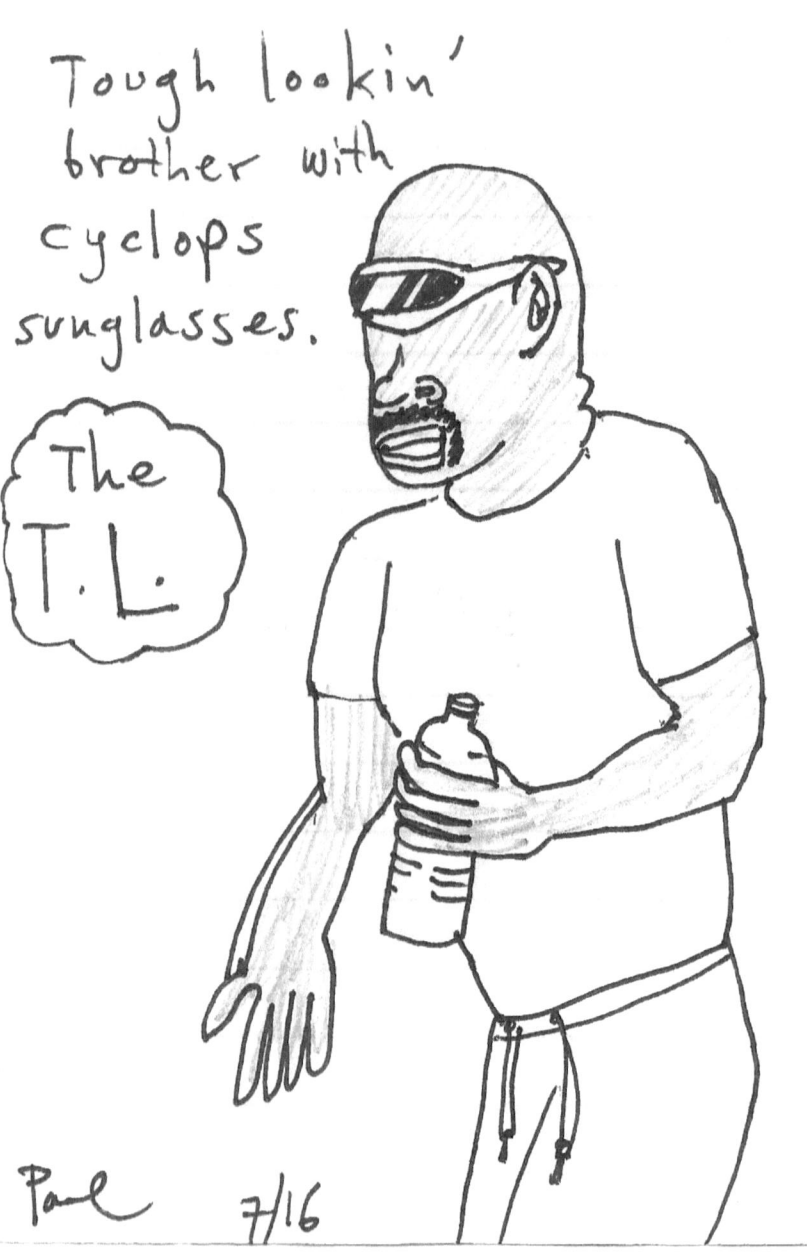

Paul   7/16

T-shirt I copied out of
a magazine and got
sent
home
for
wearing
in
high
school.

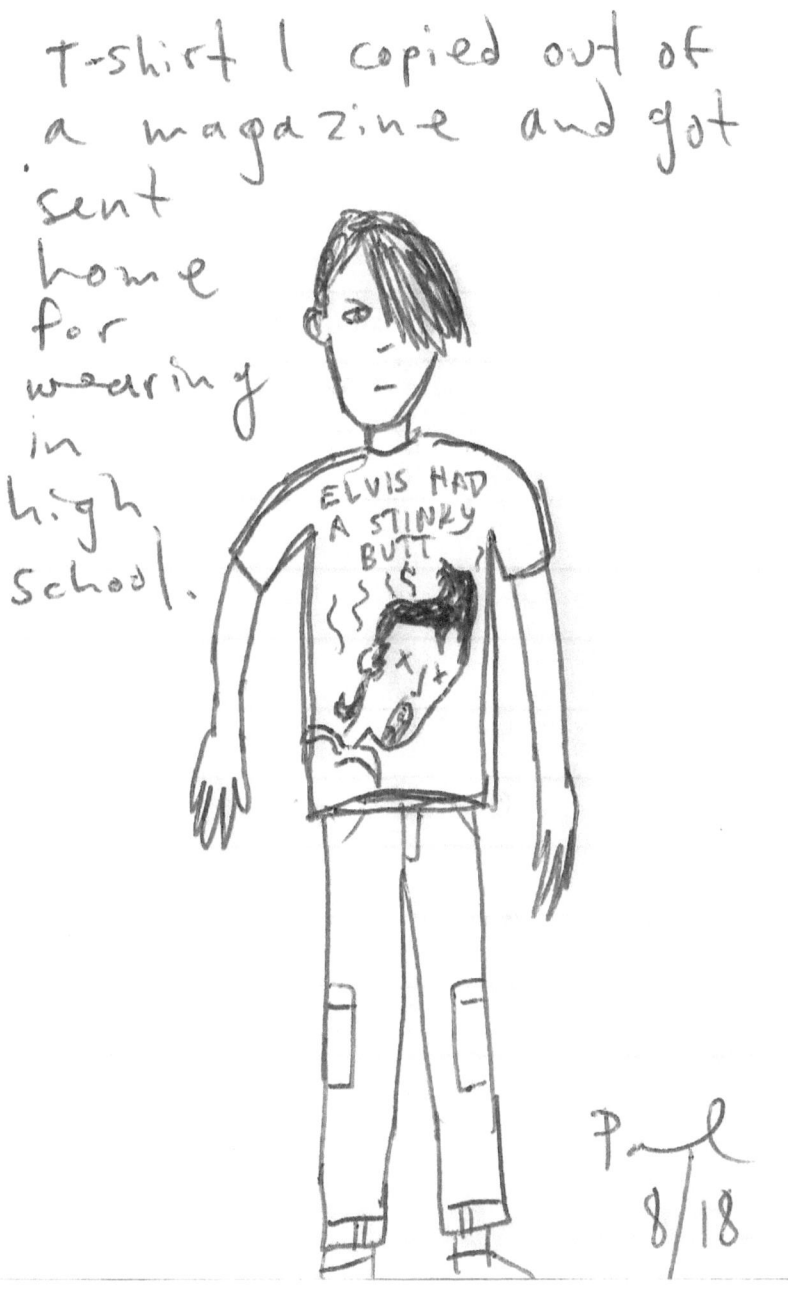

ELVIS HAD
A STINKY
BUTT

Paul
8/18

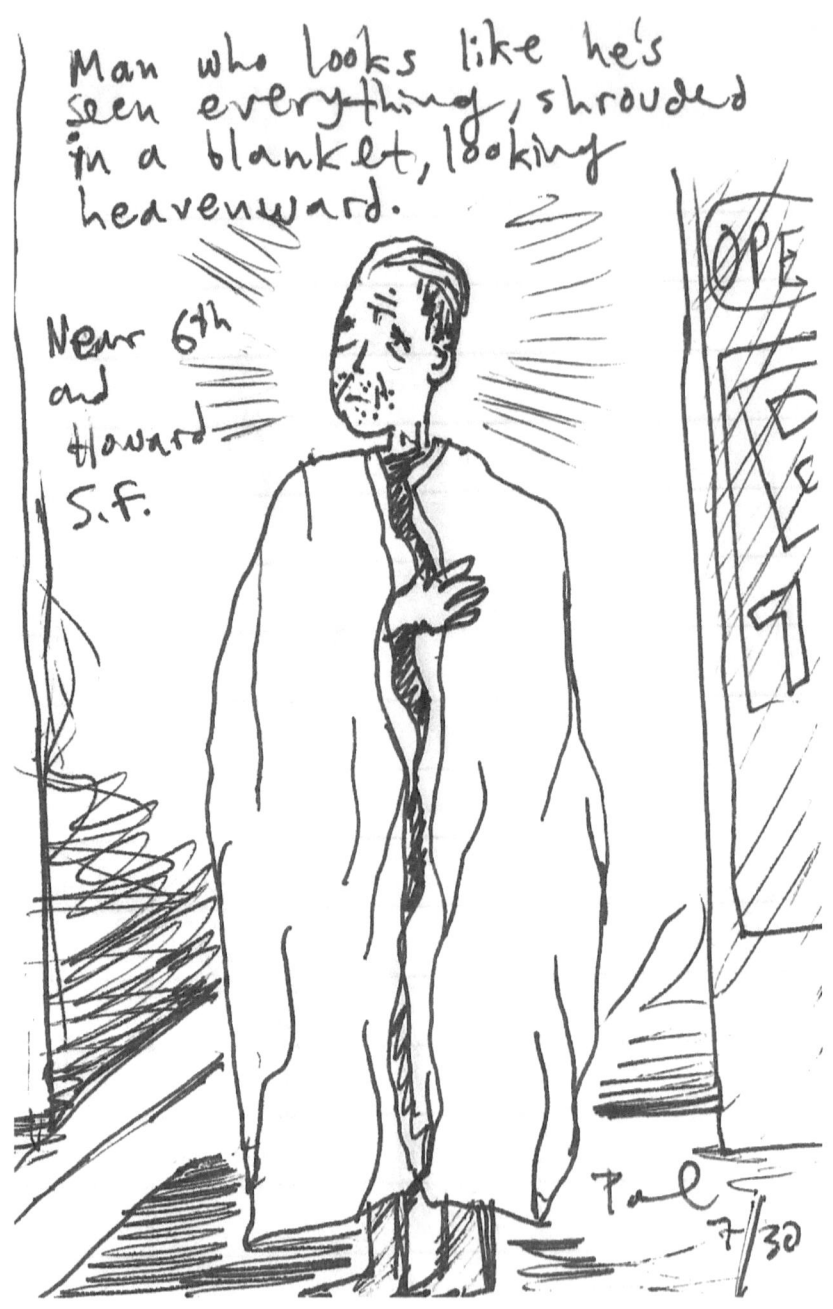

Man who looks like he's seen everything, shrouded in a blanket, looking heavenward.

Near 6th and Howard S.F.

Creepy
guy with
utility belt
furtively
smoking
a
joint
in a
doorway
near
Ritual

Paul
7/23

Mayor of
Lesbosopolis

Paul
7/23

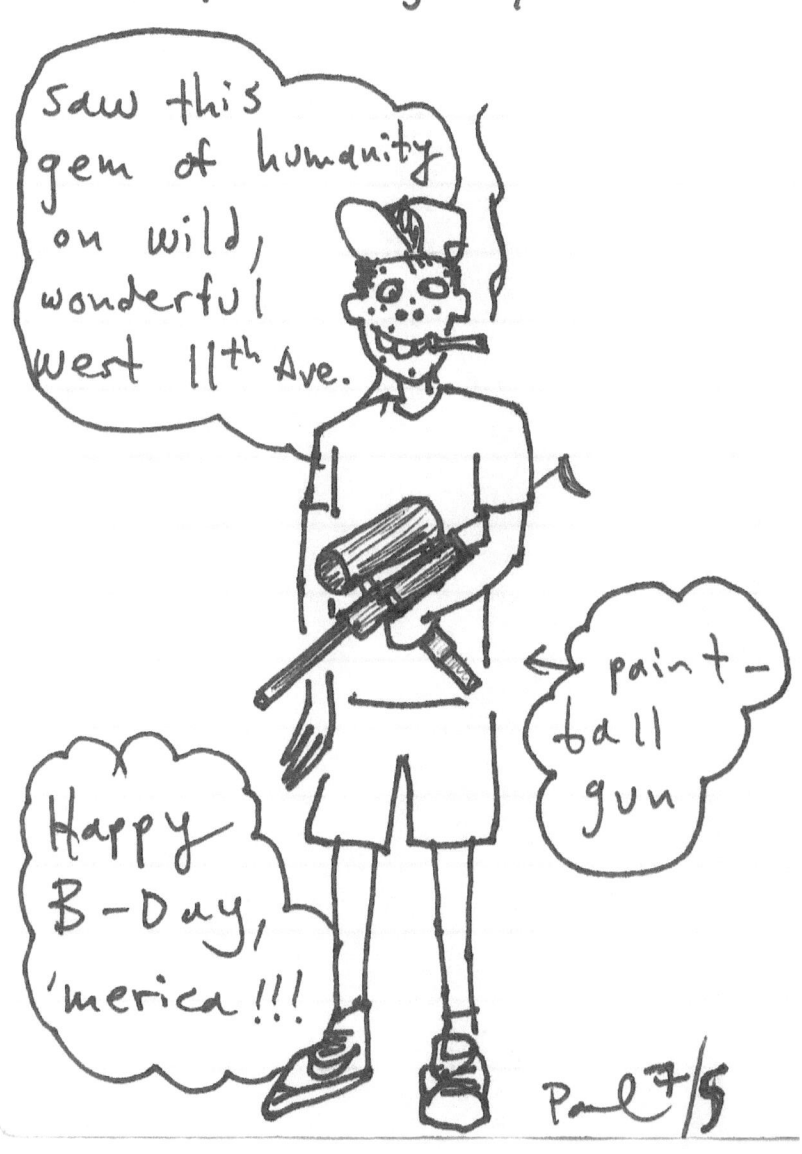

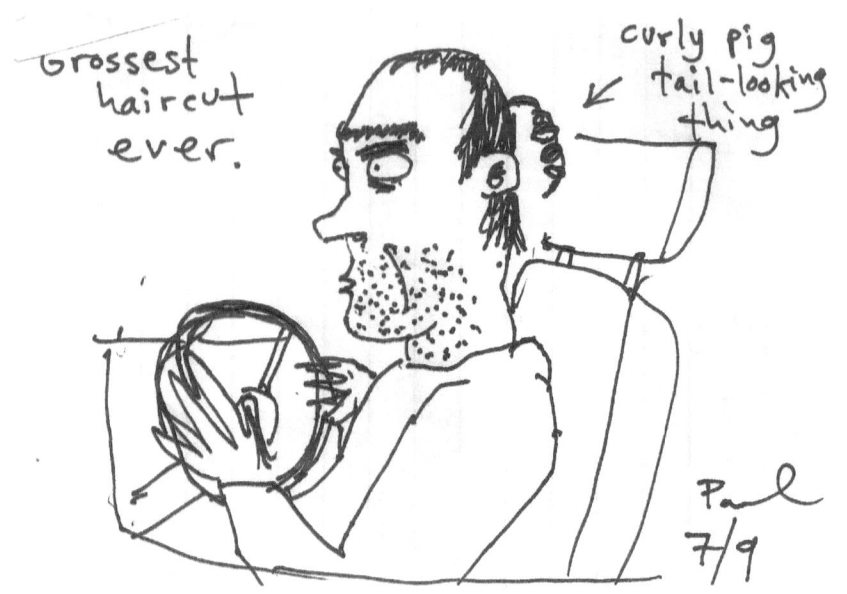

Does every city have a tall senior citizen health nut who is red from constant exposure to the elements and loves short shorts?

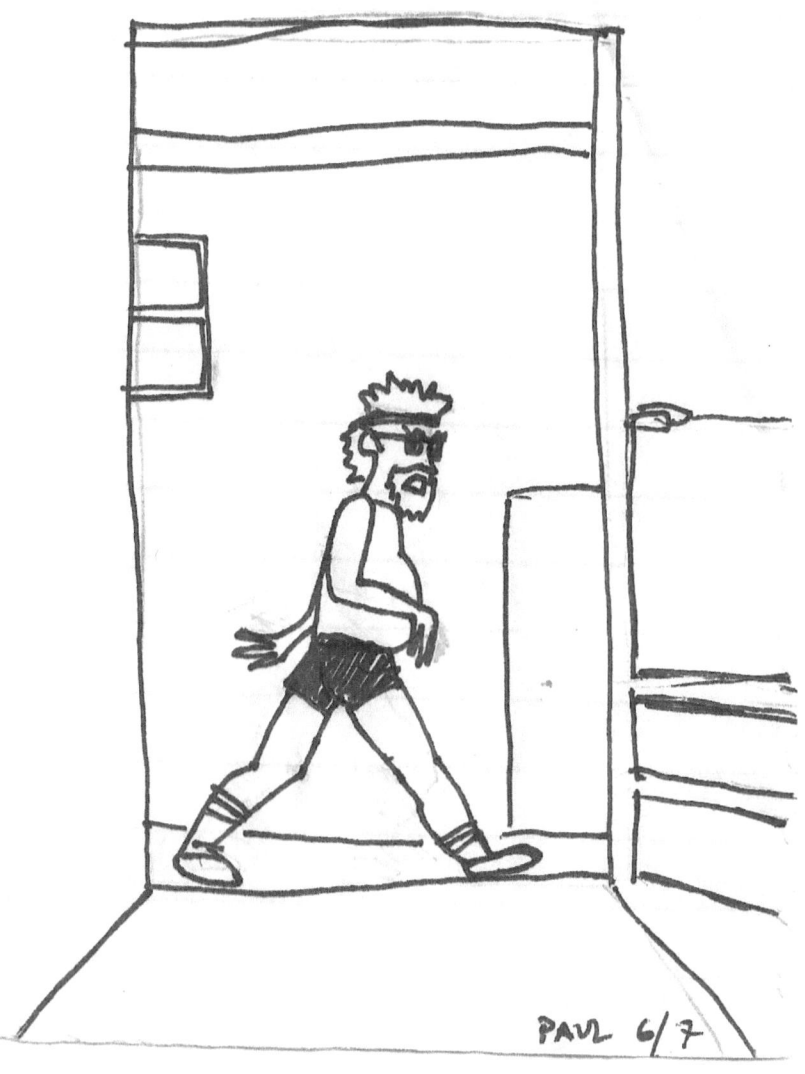

PAUL 6/7

# whole foods

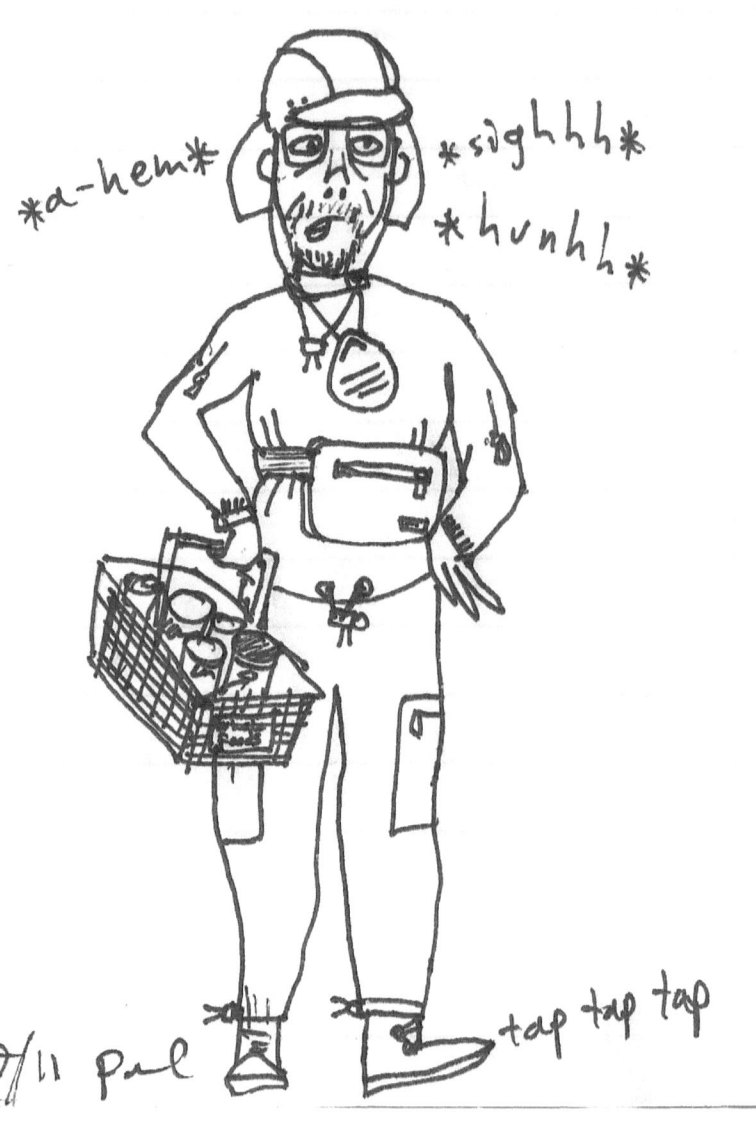

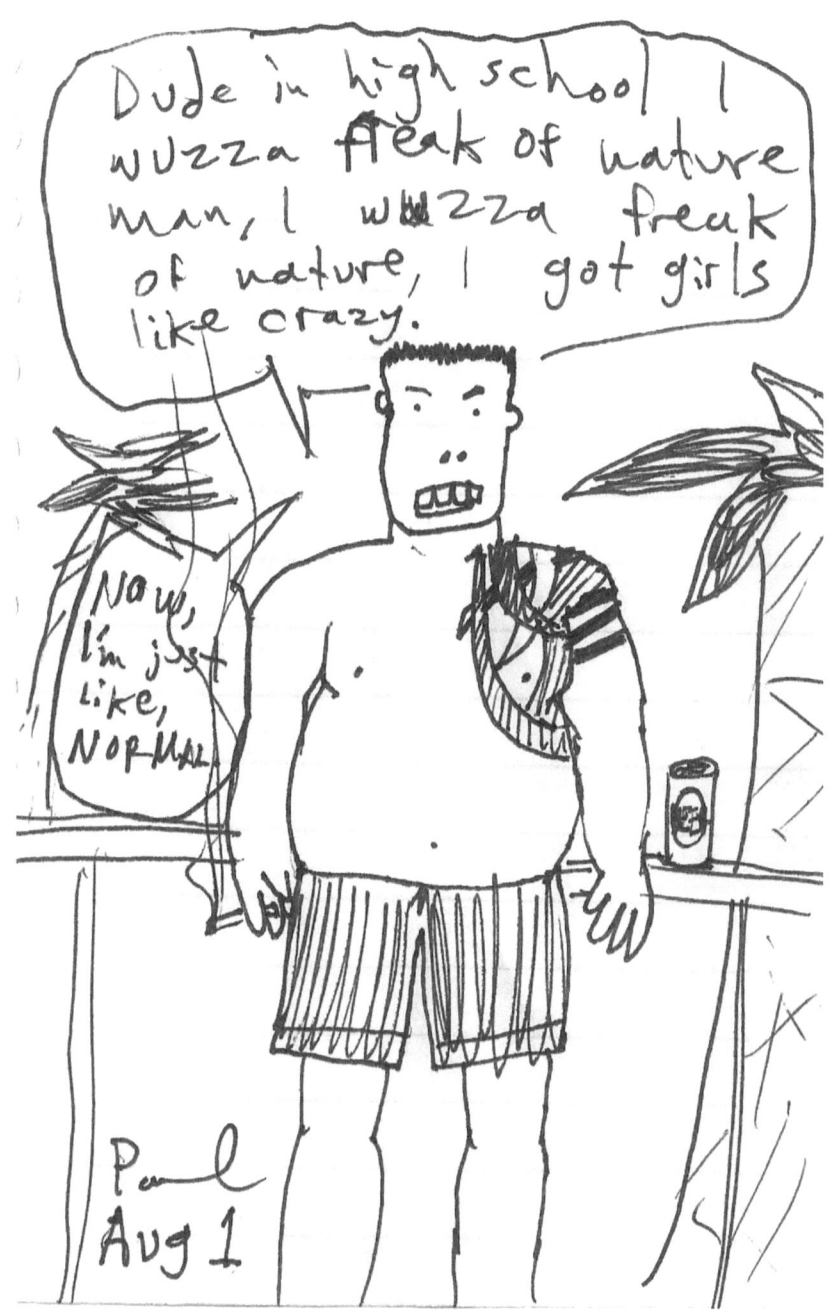

61

The exterminator
I saw prowling
around a building
near 7th and
Market.

I bet he
does some
crazy Naked
Lunch shit
with his
bug juice.

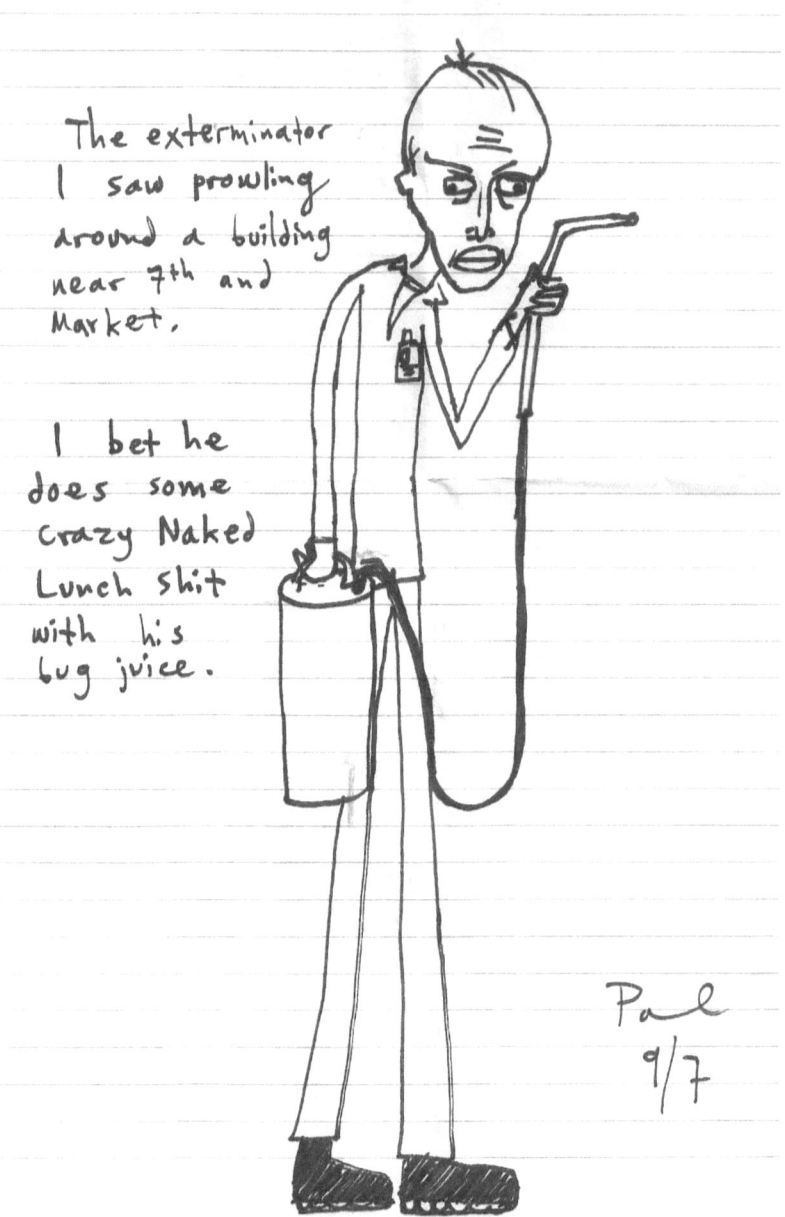

Paul
9/7

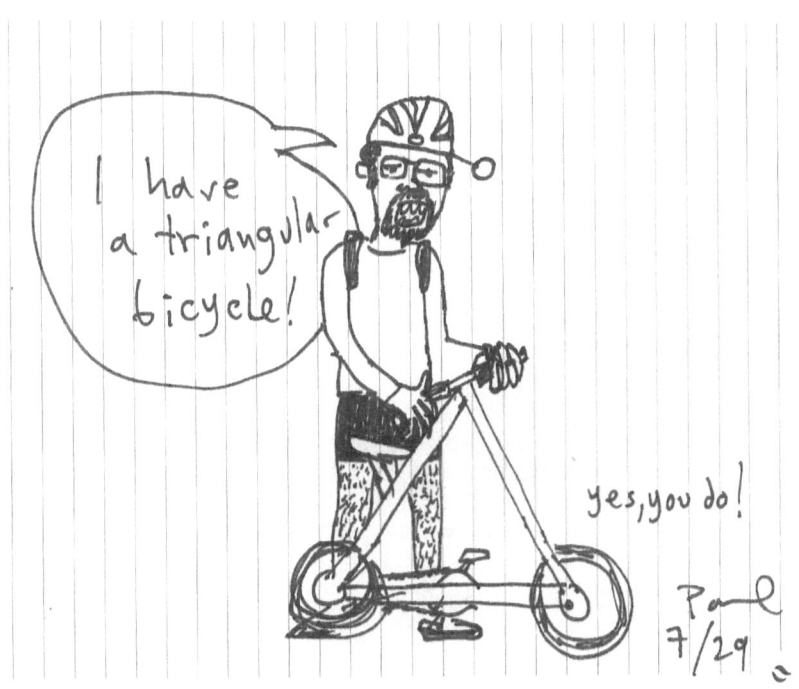

Huge gay "bear" dude
in what appeared to be
a rubber
  scuba suit.
It's 80° today
in Silver
Lake.

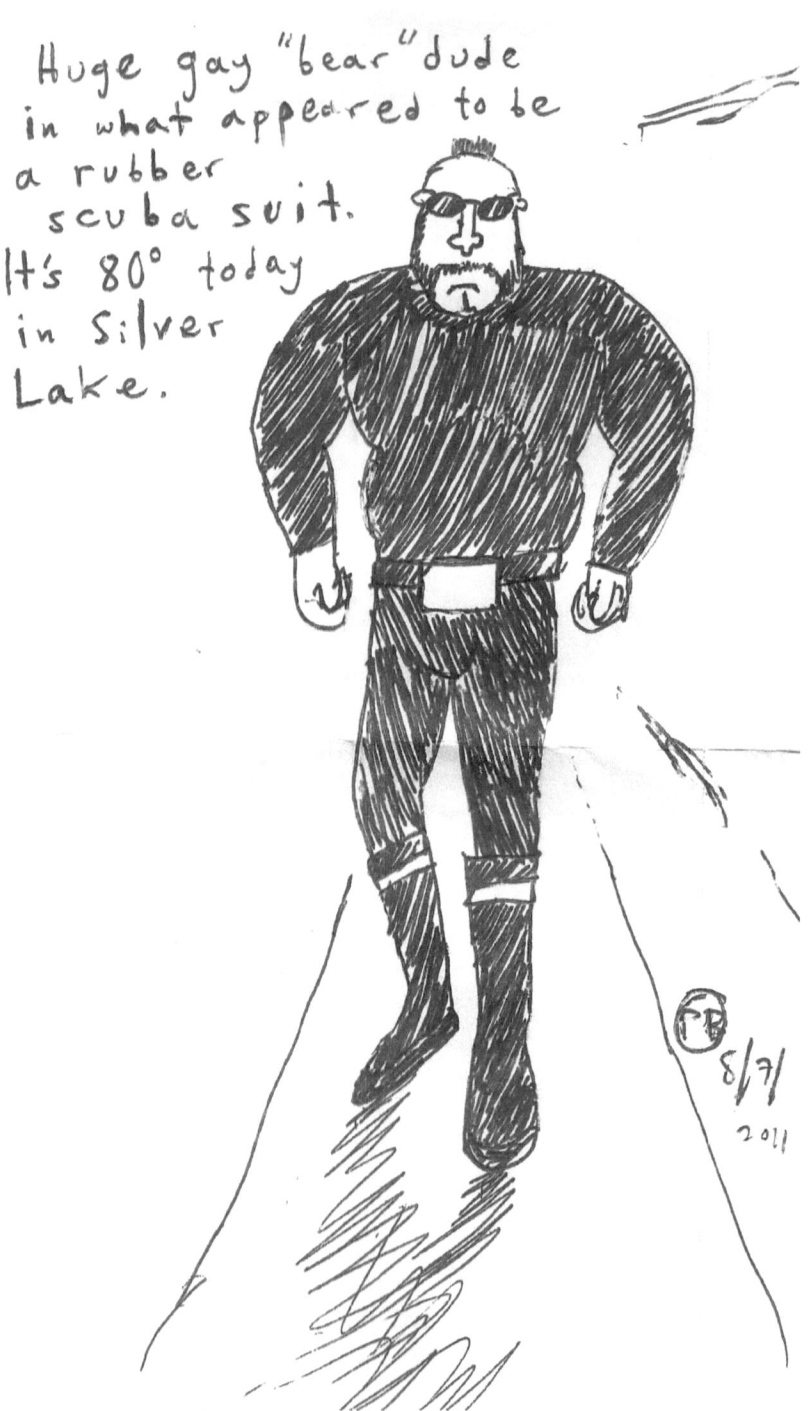

8/7/
2011

When I saw
this Dexy's
midnight
Runners dude
I laughed
out loud
at him.

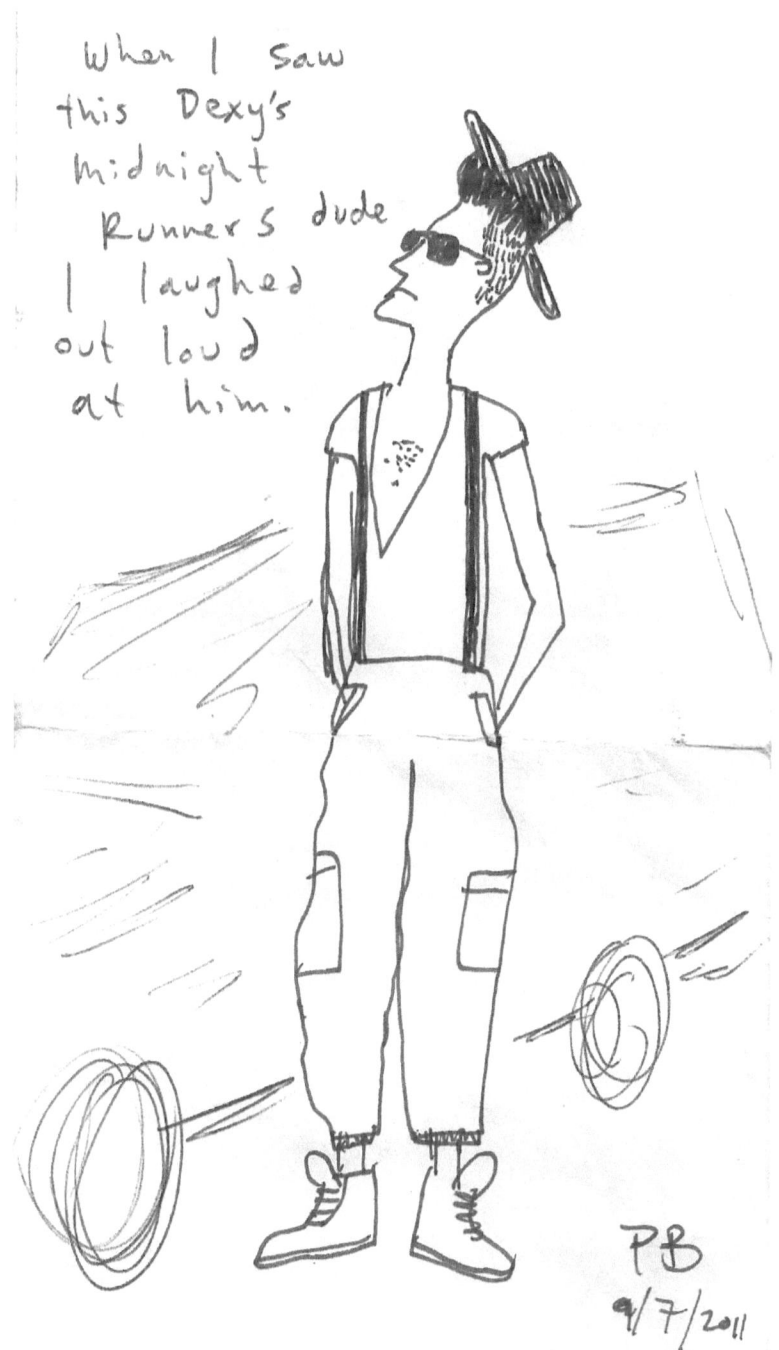

PB
9/7/2011

ON LA METRO

Thing in wig wear-
ing all black
clutching a bust
of a mannequin
dressed as
his/her twin.
Really
creepy.

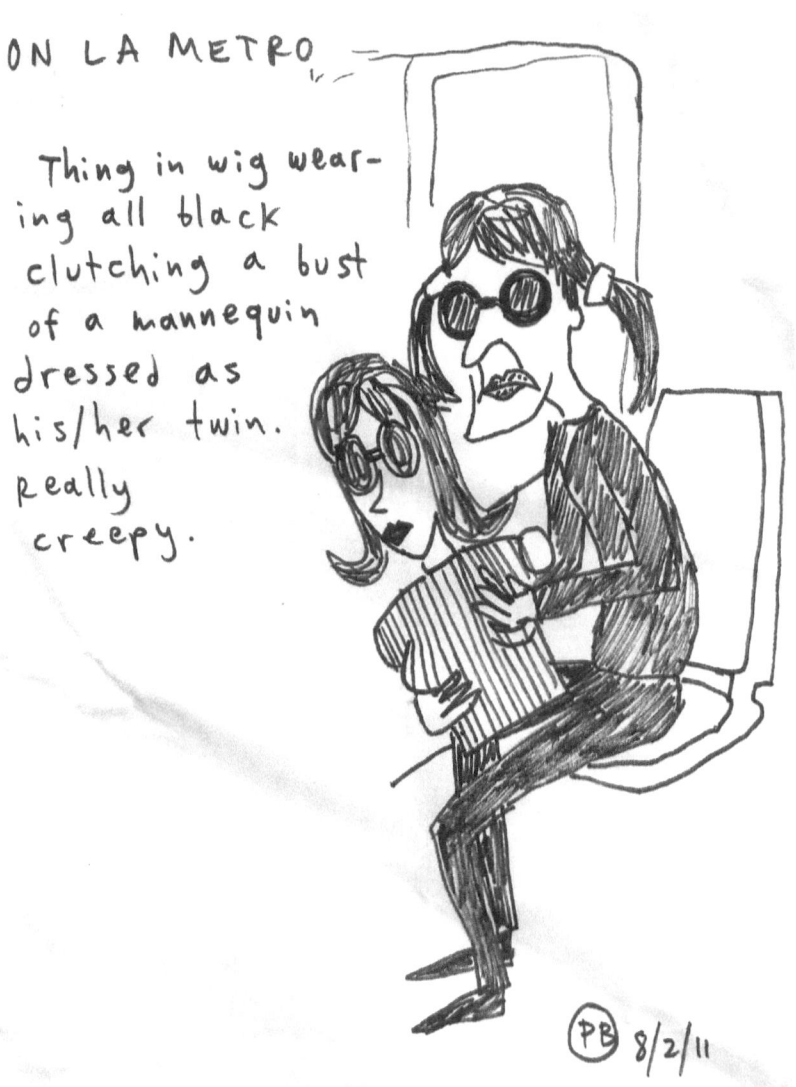

PB 8/2/11

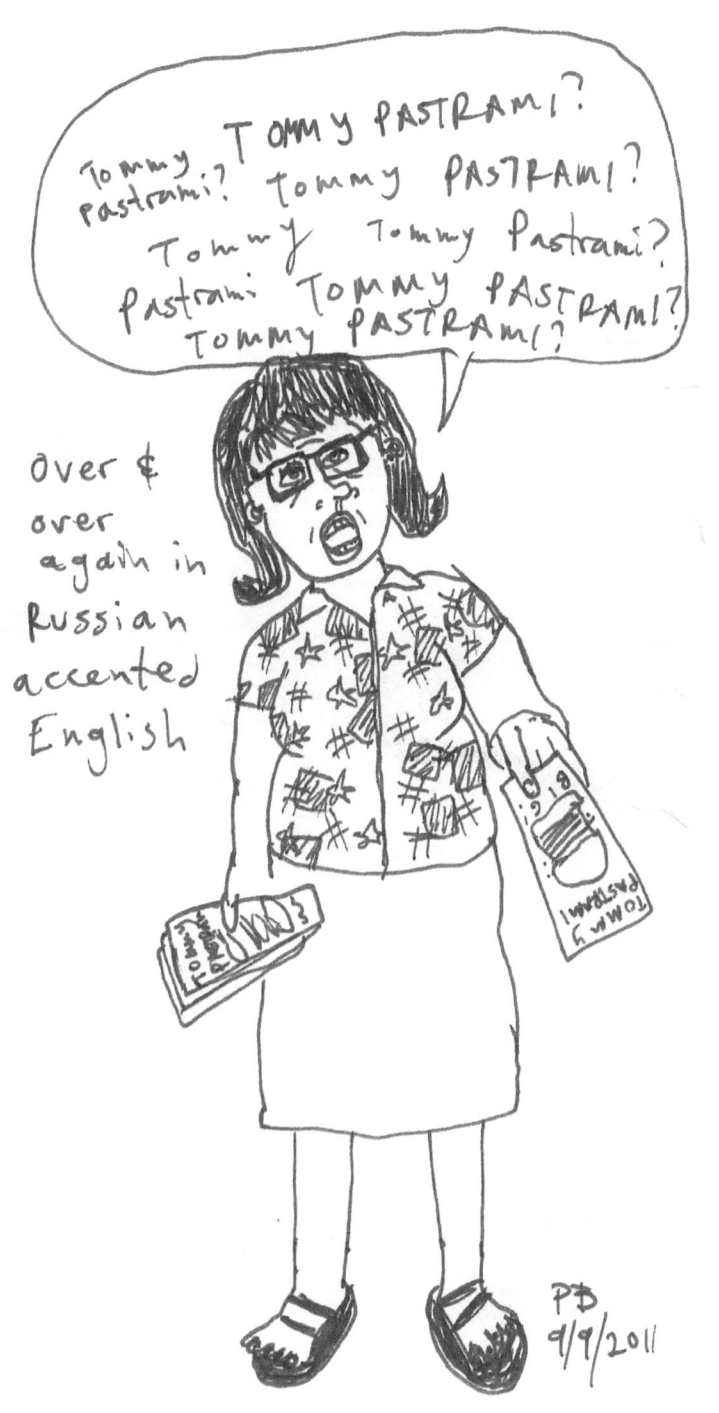

Korean
Janet Jackson
woman at
Korean BBQ
joint.
For Amy
Davis!
She had a
friend who
may have
had a
bonnet on.

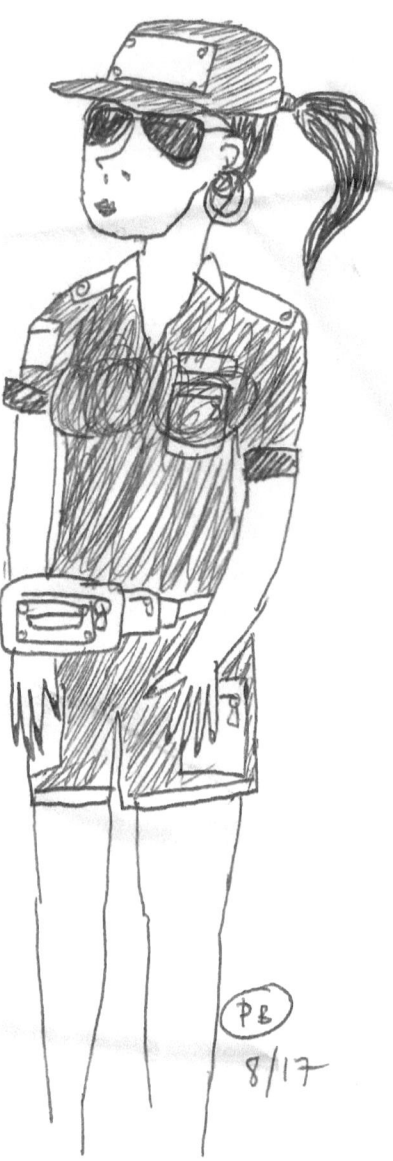

PB

8/17

Weird trannies in bad drag trying to find the subway in downtown Los Angeles. All drugged out and shit.

PB
7/20

When I saw the woman I often see roaming
around the Hollywood/Western Metro station
(in filthy clothes and talking to herself)
squatting on the sidewalk in front of
me I thought:"Oh great, she's taking
a crap." But she was only watching
a butterfly.

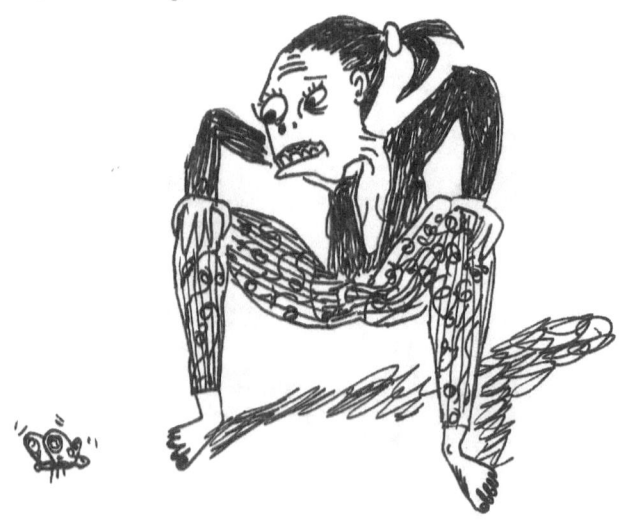

PB 6/24
/2011

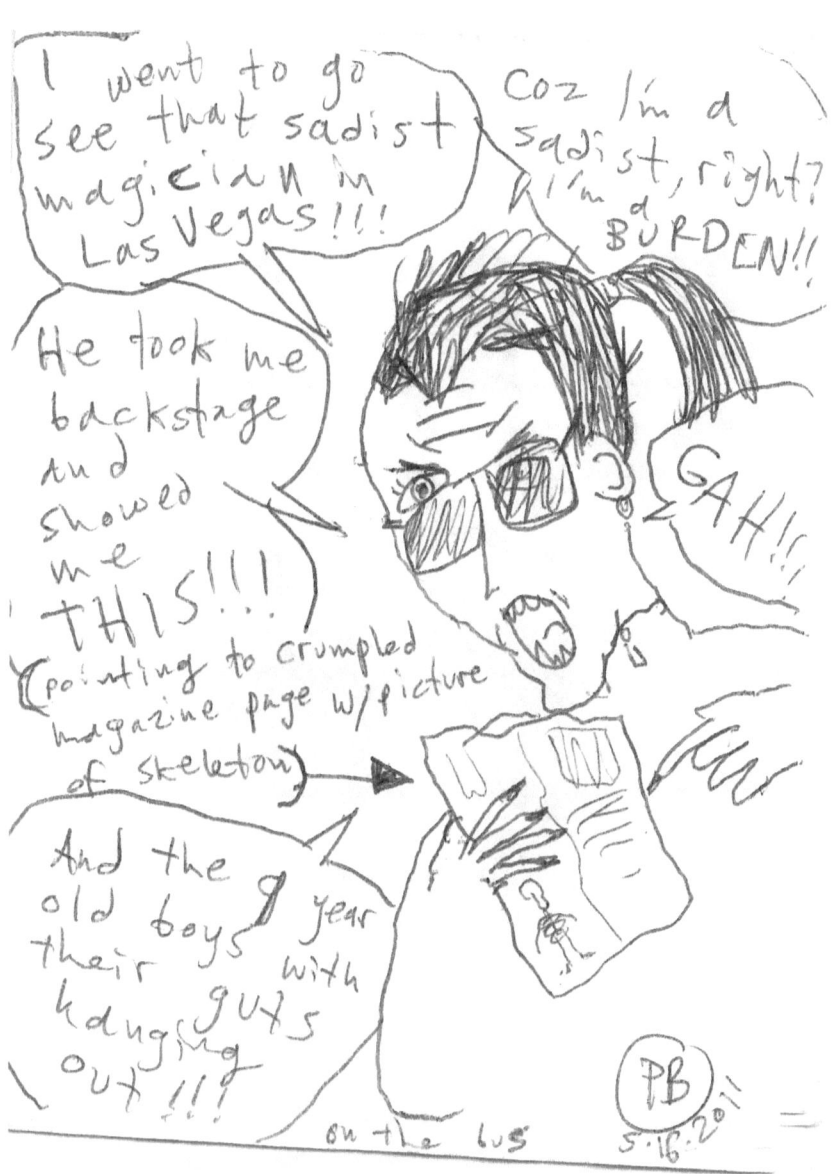

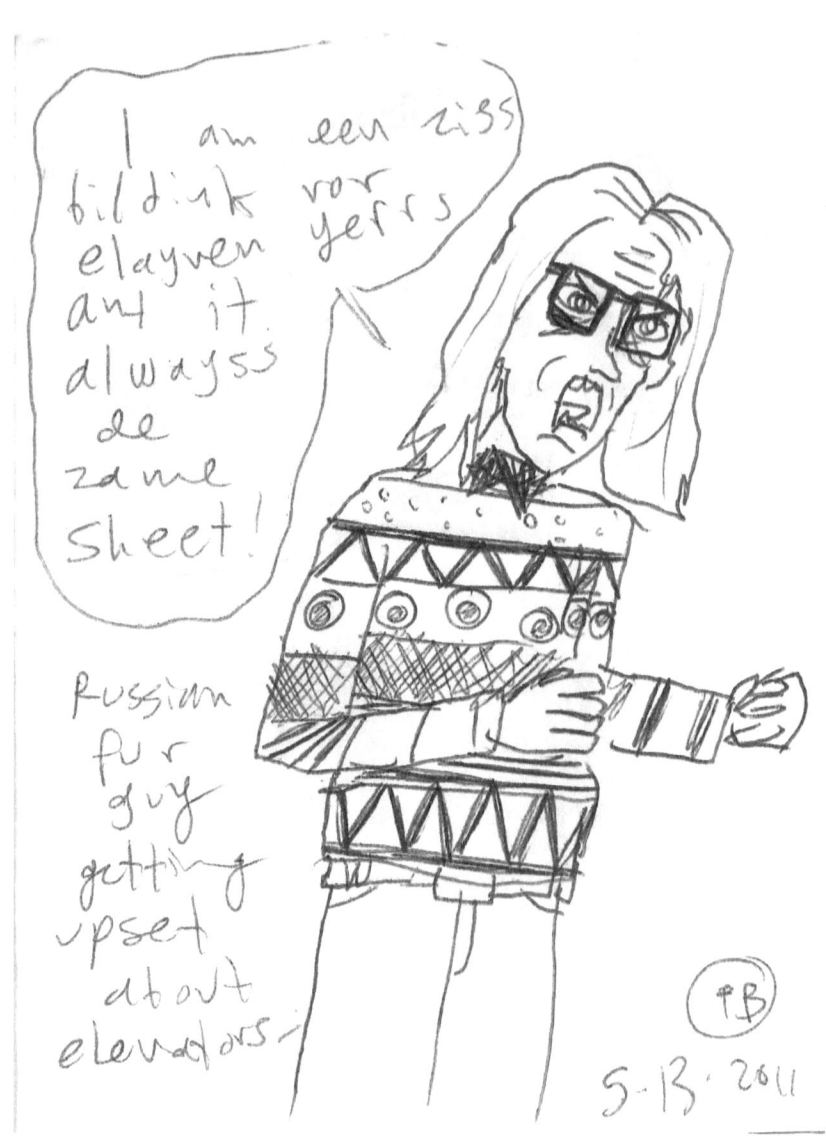

Adult man on L.A. Metro reading
book about monsters and
looking very excited

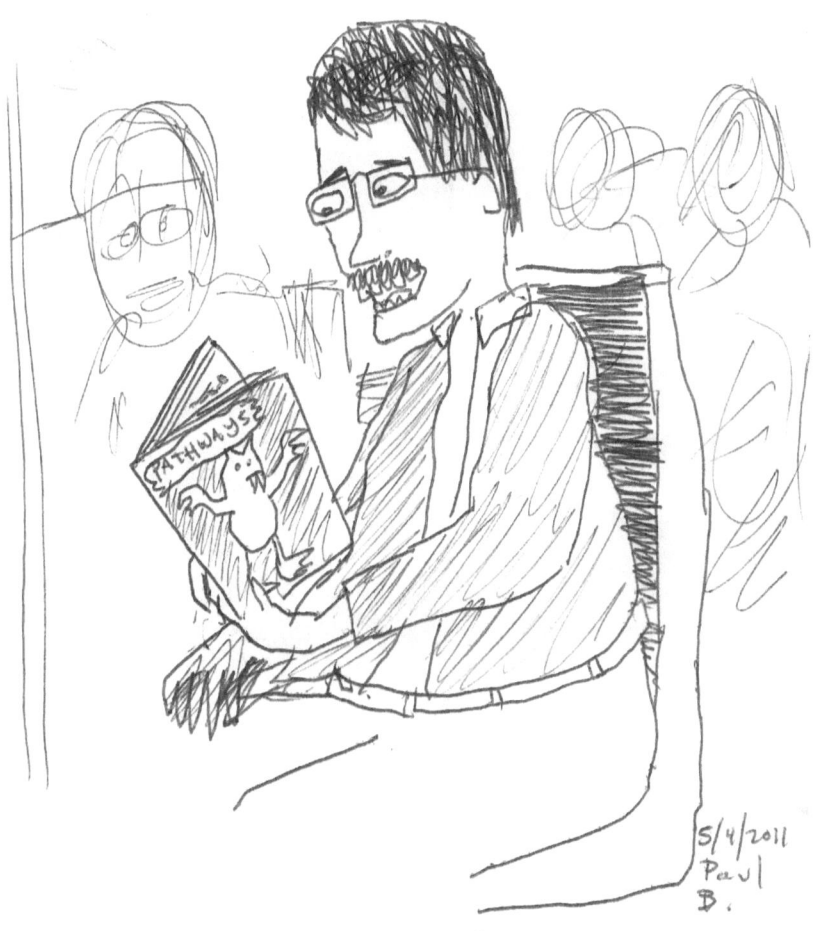

5/4/2011
Paul
B.

Often see this guy on my way to work in downtown Los Angeles.

He goes to 7-11 to fill up his giant Extreme Big Gulp cup every morning.

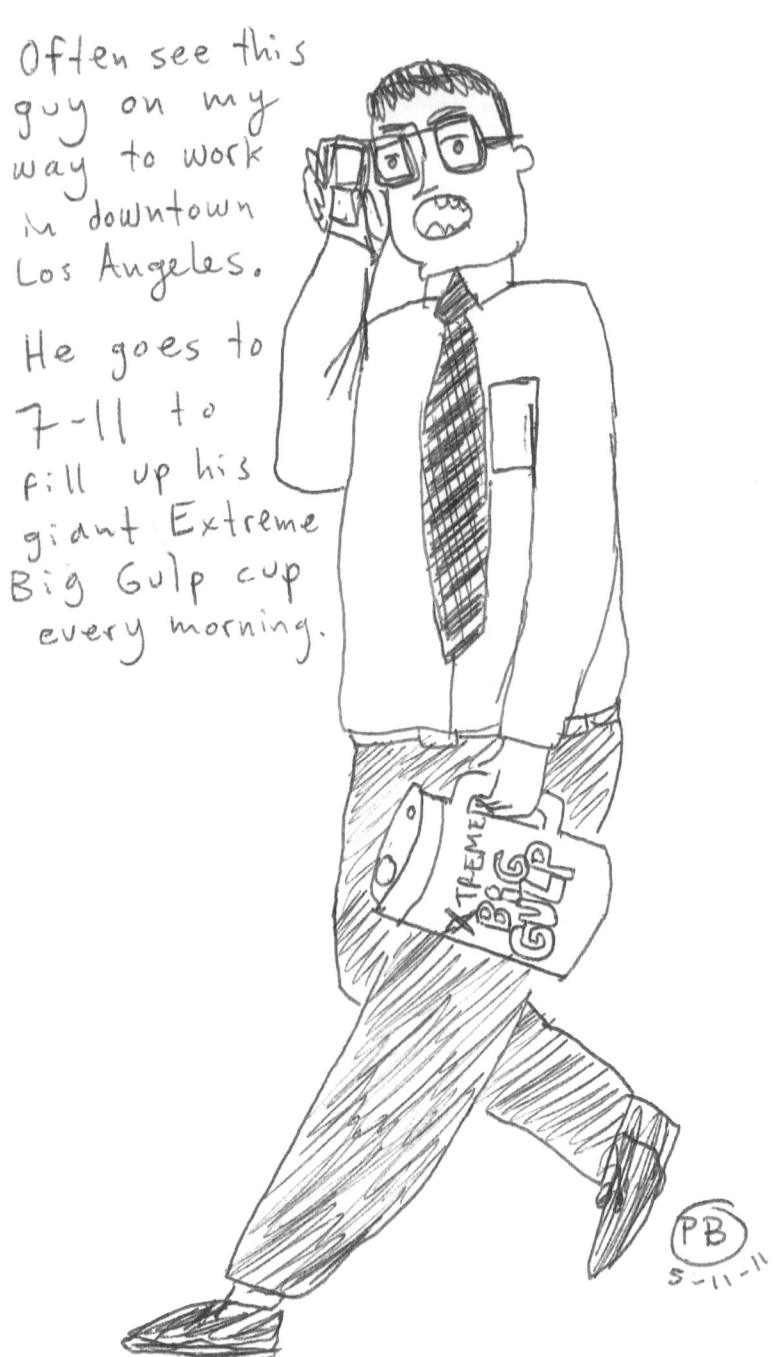

Foreign idiot
walking around
Sunset Blvd. in
Echo Park
taking pictures
with HIS
SHOELACES
TIED
TOGETHER!

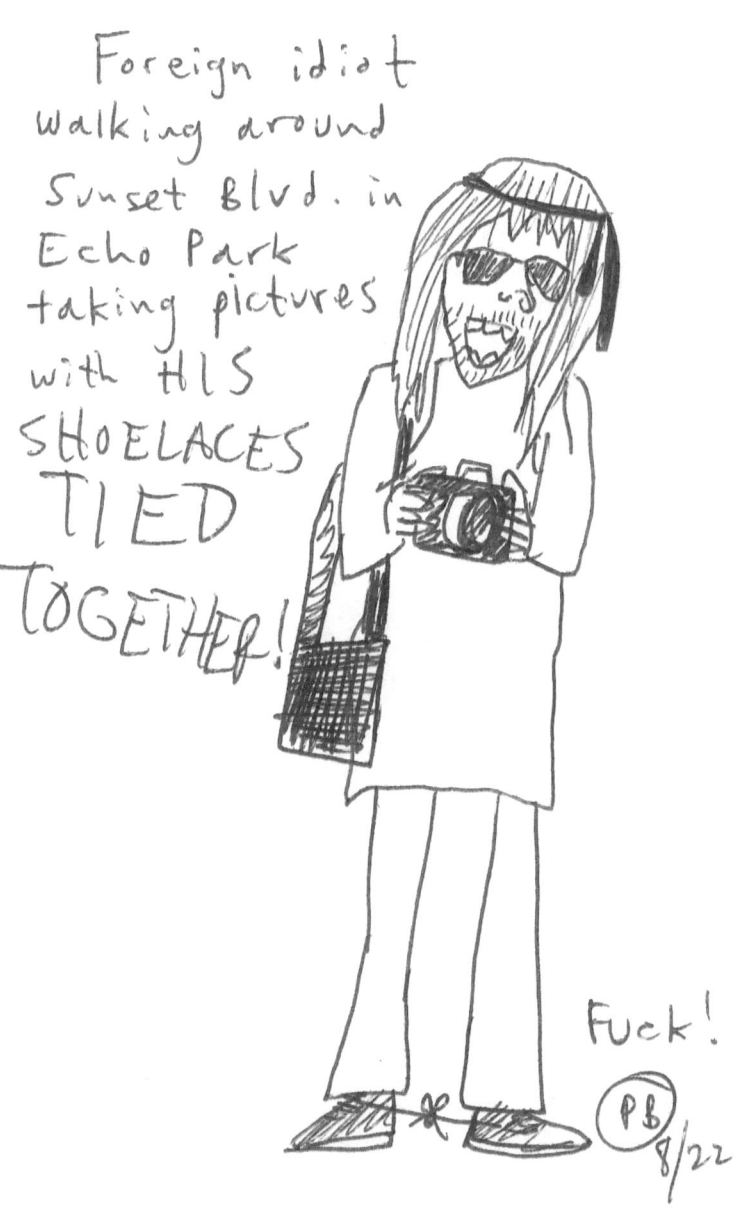

Fuck!
PB
8/22

Behind a door with a keyhole-shaped
window in the basement of an office
building in downtown Los Angeles...

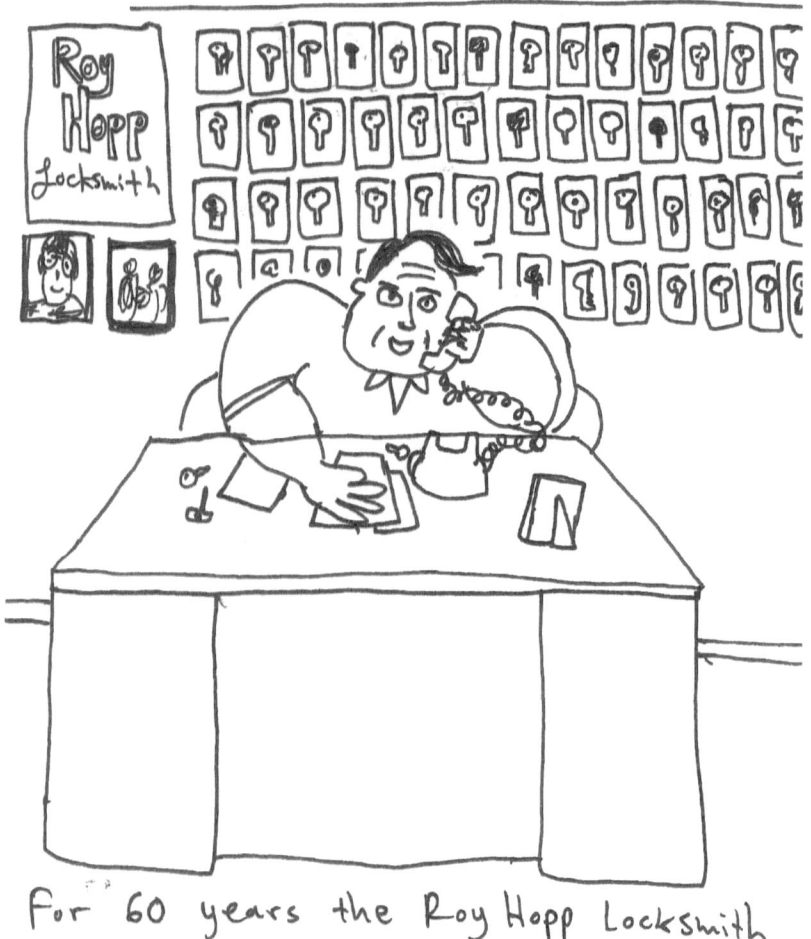

For 60 years the Roy Hopp Locksmith
company has operated out of the
same underground location.

PB  6/9/2011

Happy couple with matching Oakley
Blades, camo shorts and ipods
enjoying a promenade on Franklin.
I think I laughed out loud at
their weird expressions.
They looked hella pissed!

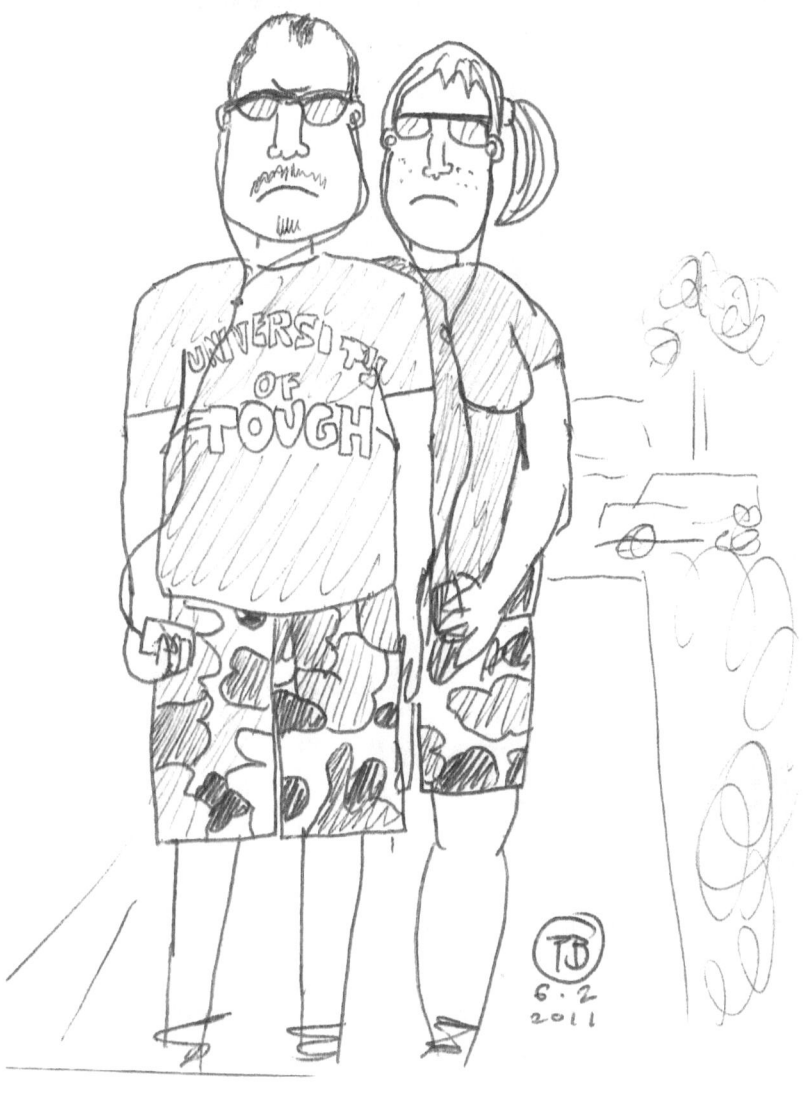

Early-morning drinker on the way to the bus stop who was grateful I returned his: "good morning!"

There aren't many of us LEFT!

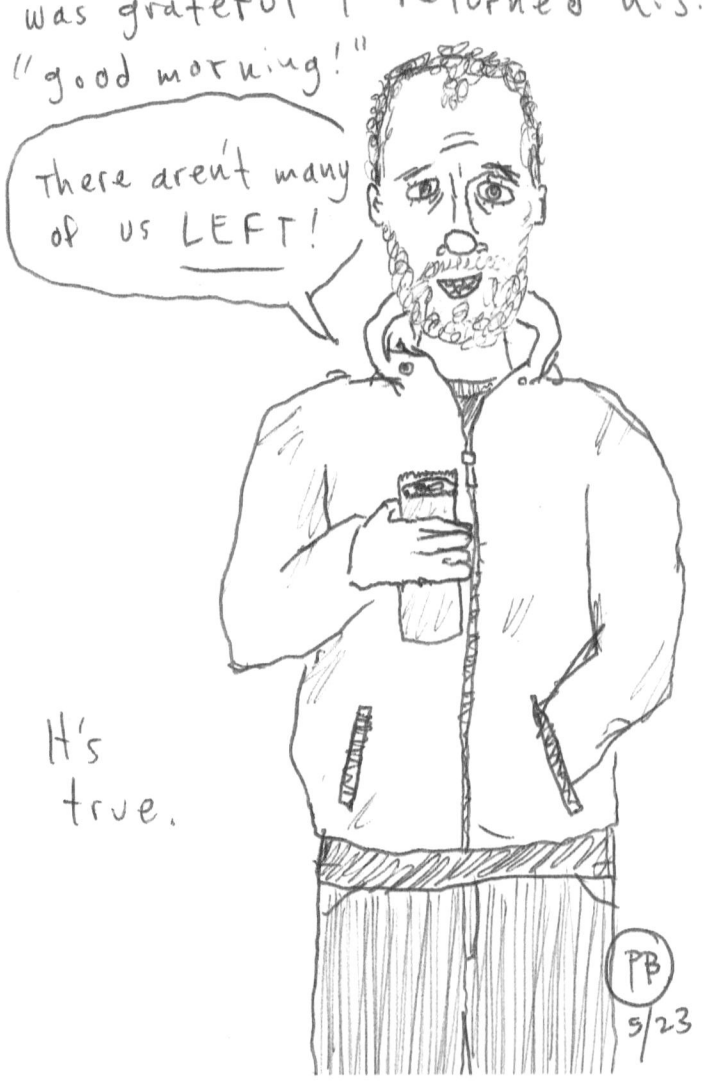

It's true.

www.ingramcontent.com/pod-product-compliance
Lightning Source LLC
Chambersburg PA
CBHW022131170526

45157CB00004B/1831